# RICHMOND FIRE DEPARTMENT

A HISTORY OF SERVICE

**M.T. Publishing Company, Inc.**
P.O. Box 6802
Evansville, Indiana 47719-6802
www.mtpublishing.com

Copyright © 2010
Richmond Fire Department

Graphic Designer: Elizabeth A. Dennis

All rights reserved. No part of this publication may be translated, reproduced, or transmitted in any form or by any means, electronic or mechanical, including photocopying and recording, or by any information storage and retrieval system, without expressed written permission of the copyright owner and M.T. Publishing Company, Inc.

The materials were compiled and produced using available information; M.T. Publishing Company, Inc., and the copyright owner regret they cannot assume liability for errors or omissions.

Library of Congress
Control Number 2010939479

ISBN: 978-1-934729-47-2

Printed in the United States
of America

# CONTENTS

Introduction to the Firefighters of the City of Richmond    5
Thank You    6
Acknowledgements    7
Line Of Duty Deaths    8
A Word From the Fire Chief    14
Mission Statement    15
Chiefs of RFD    16
Richmond Fire Department History    19
Apparatus Through the Years    32
Richmond Fire Department Fire Stations    39
Closed Fire Houses & Disbanded Companies    102
Badges of the Richmond Fire Department    103
Administration    104
Fire Prevention Division    106
Investigations Unit    110
Fire Training Division    114
Communications    118
Richmond Fire Department Personnel    121
    Fire Chief    122
    Deputy Chiefs    122
    Battalion Chiefs    123
    Chaplain    123
    Officers    124
    Firefighters    127
    Administrative Staff    137
    Retirees    138
Station Life    139
Notable Events    142
Man's Best Friend    148
MDA & Jerry's Kids    149
Index    150
Firefighter's Career History    152

*Doorway to Hell!*

# Introduction to the Firefighters of the City of Richmond

For over 200 years, men and women of all races and backgrounds have stepped forward and placed their lives in danger to serve and protect the lives and property of the citizens of the City of Richmond and surrounding areas. Though this great city has seen tremendous growth in population and service area, the Richmond Fire volunteers, Bureau, and eventually Department has evolved to continuously meet the needs of its citizens in a courteous and professional manner. The members of the department are as diverse as the city itself and yet the values of a firefighter have remained unchanged over the many years. When a firefighter takes their oath of service, they vow not only to protect, but to remain honorable, loyal, trustworthy, courageous, capable, and strong of character. These brave men and women endure great sacrifice when duty calls and do not hesitate to do whatever it takes to get the job done as safely and effectively as possible. From the heat of summer to the frigid cold of winter, at any hour day or night , these individuals can be relied on to aid those in need whatever the situation may be.

*Firefighter Roger R. Myers, Editor, and family*

From childhood we learn to trust the firefighters who are always there to help us and as adults who have joined this great profession, we continue the traditions and standards set by those who came before us. We honor the lives of past members in the performance of our duties and a job well done. In decades past, brave men and women fought raging fires armed only with buckets of water passed hand to hand over great distances in hopes of saving whatever possible. Today's firefighters, armed with modern equipment and specialized training now have the capability to greatly reduce public loss both in lives and property. Past wildland and house fires have evolved into high rise multi-unit and commercial fires.

The ever present threat of terrorism brings with it the possibility of attack using chemical, biological, and radiological agents. Training for the modern firefighter is ongoing as new methods of building construction and materials have created many new hazards to encounter. On September 11th, 2001 an attack on the Twin Towers of the World Trade Center in New York City took the lives of 343 New York City firefighters and many other first responders thus driving home the need for enhancing the capabilities of the fire service and the need to broaden the scope and responsibilities of its members. Richmond's firefighters are trained not only to fight fires but to respond to medical, swiftwater incidents, hazardous materials, technical rescue, acts of terrorism, and many other types of emergencies.

In the year 2008 the United States suffered with a decline in the economy not seen since the "Great Depression". The Fire Service nation wide fell victim to severe budget cuts and staffing shortages adding to the dangers faced by its firefighters. The inability to replace aging apparatus, purchase new equipment, and fill staffing vacancies increased the workload and demanded more of an already weary force. Still, its members endure, serving ever proudly in the face of adversity as has been the case over the past 200 years.

This book is dedicated to the many men and women of Richmond's Fire Service and their families. It is also a tribute to those over the years who paid the ultimate sacrifice in service of others. While gone, they never will be forgotten. Their spirit lives in the hearts of today's members and in the pages of this book. To our families we thank you for all the support, love, sacrifice, and understanding. You are the guiding force that allows us to persevere in the tasks that lay before us. It is my hope that the pages to follow will bring back memories, educate, enlighten, and bring as much joy to you as I received in helping with its creation.

Roger R. Myers, Jr.
Editor

# THANK YOU

*Captain Keith Vida, Committee Head, Kimberli Russ Vida, RFD Foundation, and their children*

A couple of years ago as the Richmond Fire Department was approaching its 150th anniversary the idea came up for a commemorative book. When you are the 6th oldest professional fire department in the United States you should celebrate this fact, so I was understandably excited about the idea of our department building a historical document of which we could all be proud. I will be the first to tell you I did not have a clue about the amount of work that goes into producing a commemorative book. This project, that I thought would take about a year, has instead taken us almost two to complete. The members of the yearbook committee have spent countless hours conducting research, writing articles, and gathering pictures for this book. While I am truly grateful for the yearbook committee's dedication and help, I would especially like to thank Roger Myers (our editor), retired Captain John Hinant, and Tommy Herman for all of their hard work. Roger has spent hundreds of hours gathering pictures and information, and putting this book together. John Hinant was involved in the last yearbook produced by the department in 1992, and has been extremely helpful in providing accurate historical information about our department.

Tommy Herman is in a category all by himself. Tommy spent thirteen years as a Richmond firefighter before leaving and going into the fire sprinkler industry. He has collected information, pictures, fire trucks, and about anything else you can think of from Virginia's fire service for over 30 years, but has always had a fondness for the Richmond Fire Department. His collection is easily the single largest source of information and history of the Richmond Fire Department in the country, and I say this without seeing anyone else's collection! When the Valentine Museum needed an expert for their exhibit on our department last year they called Tommy. So naturally we tapped into this unparalleled resource as well. Tommy was kind enough to open and grant us access to his extensive collection. The first time we went through Tommy's collection we asked questions like "Do you have anything on Truck Station 2?" We quickly learned the appropriate question was "Where is the information on Truck Station 2?" So thanks to the lifelong commitment and passion for the fire service, this book contains information, pictures, and posters from Tommy's collection, many of which have never been published before. I hope you are as excited to see these pictures as I was the first time I saw them. We wanted to

 ## ACKNOWLEDGEMENTS

Special thanks go out to those who graciously donated their photos, articles, literature, insight, time, and effort. To all those who gave access to private collections and family heirlooms, without your help this book could never have come to be. Thank you so very much.

Thomas Herman Collection
Captain John Hinant (Retired)
John F. Finnegan Family Collection
Dr. Walter S. Griggs Jr.
Captain William Beatley
Mike Legeros (www.Legeros.com)
FF Melvin Cash Collection
FF George Bridgers
Captain Carroll Smith (Retired)
Lieutenant Shawn Jones
Lieutenant Dave Burns (Retired)
FF Wesley Taylor
FF Dan Waldron
FF Roger Walker
William J. Perdue
Library of Congress
Valentine Richmond History Center
*Richmond Times Dispatch*
*Richmond News Leader*
*History of the Providence Stage*, 1762-1891, page 50
*The New York Times*, New York, NY 7 Sept 1869
*The Philadelphia Inquirer*, Philadelphia PA 28 Apr 1870
*The Sun*, Baltimore, MD 11 Oct 1915
*The Miami Herald*, Miami, FL 28 Feb 1922
*Richmond Fire Bureau Yearbook 1992*

And the many others not mentioned who also contributed in some way to this project.

Founded on the principles that continue to make the Richmond Fire Department's Credit Union an integral support to firefighters and their families, their charter was formed on May 11, 1929. It started with three firefighters pooling their money to help a fellow firefighter purchase a sewing machine. This single act of support spring boarded into establishing the same opportunity for all members. Fast forward 79 years and this legacy has grown into a $14,000,000 dollar corporation with over 1,300 members across the United States and throughout the world.

But walking through their door, you are met with the personalized service and attention of a small town bank. They proved once again no matter how large or small the task, or even if it is a rather unusual request, as this commemorative book was, they are always available to help. With the credit union taking over the responsibility of the financial issues and order taking, Roger and I were able to concentrate on producing this publication. We greatly appreciate their assistance in making this commemorative book a reality.

### History Book Committee

Captain Keith Vida - Committee Head
Firefighter Roger Myers - Editor
Captain John Hinant (retired)
Firefighter Tommy L. Herman (retired)
Captain Rob Baumgardner
Firefighter Charles Bridgers
Firefighter Ronald Edwards Jr.
Captain Pat Schoeffel
Firefighter Stewart Thiel
Kimberli Russ Vida - RFD Foundation
Firefighter Anthony Wells

# LINE OF DUTY DEATHS

## THE FALLEN

*A life spent in service, a soul that truly cared,
Lives touched, lives helped, lives changed, lives saved.
Because my brother, you were there.
For those that did not know you, I speak of you with pride,
To have you as my friend, and standing by my side.
Like a shining star you graced us, like a falling star you left us.
We laughed, we cried, we played, we worked,
Till duty's call would break us.
Gone but not forgotten, your memory forges on.
The deeds you've done, the hearts you touched,
Marks every battle won.
Now as you look down from heaven,
We carry on your fight.
There is no doubt for the life you've lived,
You've earned your rest tonight.*

Roger R. Myers Jr.

# LINE OF DUTY DEATHS

### William Ligon
**August 20, 1854**
Firefighter – Engine Company No. 5

Killed in the line of duty by a falling wall at the Enders Tobacco Warehouse.

### Nicholas Walsh
**August 20, 1854**
Firefighter – Engine Company No. 3

Killed in the line of duty by a falling wall at the Enders Tobacco Warehouse.

### W. A. Charters
**April 27, 1870**
Fire Chief
Virginia State Capitol

Chief Charters died in the line of duty when the floor that he was standing on collapsed down onto the floor below. A Mayoralty case had attracted hundreds of spectators to the Court of Appeals onto a poorly constructed 2$^{nd}$ floor addition when it suddenly collapsed onto the floor below, killing 58 and injuring over two hundred.

### E. M. Wright
**June 21, 1906**
Firefighter
610 E. Broad Street
*Evening Journal Office*

Killed in the line of duty while operating at a building fire. Shocked by a telephone wire that sent him "hurling" to the pavement. A thunderstorm had come through the area causing the wires to cross, starting a small fire on top of the *Evening Journal Office*. Wright was the first one up the ladder that was placed against the building and began extinguishing the fire when his left hand came into contact with the telephone wire, shocking him and causing him to fall to the pavement below.

### George C. Shaw
**November 21, 1908**
Chief
S. 15th Street
W. C. Boyd Baking Powder Plant

Killed in the line of duty after being overcome by smoke at the W. C. Boyd Baking Powder Plant. The Chief was taken back to Truck No. 2's house where he died shortly after.

### Charles H. Reintz
**January 18, 1912**
Lieutenant – Truck Company No. 4
811 E. Marshall Street
Binswager & Company

Lt. Reintz was killed in the line of duty fighting a fire in the Binswager & Company building (made sashes, doors, windows, glass, and mirrors). Reports are that Lt. Reintz was killed by a falling brick wall. Lt. Reintz was working with Laddermen Woodward and called for Woodward to jump when he saw the wall falling but it was too late for both of them. Woodward was injured but survived the accident. Weather conditions were said to be so cold that the only water that could be accessed to fight the fire was by a hole cut in the ice of the canal.

### Thomas H. Pegram
**July 19, 1915**
Fire Chief's Chauffeur
Brook Road & Broad Street

Killed in the line of duty when he attempted to pass another vehicle on Broad Street on the way to a small fire in a meat market on W. Broad Street. He swerved onto the sidewalk where he struck a light pole and was thrown through the windshield.

# Line of Duty Deaths

### John H. Mann
**July 19, 1915**
**Fire Commissioner**
**Brook Road & Broad Street**

Killed in the line of duty while responding to a small fire in a meat market on W. Broad Street when the vehicle he was riding in struck a light pole.

### C. L. Atkinson
**October 10, 1915**
**Firefighter – Engine Company No. 1**
**Near 13th and Virginia Streets**
**Crenshaw Warehouse**

Killed in the line of duty by a falling wall while fighting a fire at the Crenshaw Warehouse. Firefighter Atkinson was transported to a local hospital where he died of his injuries.

### R. M. Norment
**October 10, 1915**
**Captain – Engine Company No. 1**
**Near 13th and Virginia Streets**
**Crenshaw Warehouse**

Killed in the line of duty by a falling wall while fighting a fire at the Crenshaw Warehouse. Capt. Norment was killed instantly when the wall fell.

### W. R. Odell
**October 10, 1915**
**Firefighter – Engine Company No. 1**
**Near 13th and Virginia Streets**
**Crenshaw Warehouse**

Killed in the line of duty by a falling wall while fighting a fire at the Crenshaw Warehouse. Firefighter Odell was transported to a local hospital where he died of his injuries.

### M. B. Nash
**September 17, 1916**
**Engineer – Engine Company No. 5**
**201 W. Marshall Street**
**Richmond Dairy Company**

Engineer Nash, 37, was killed in the line of duty while fighting a fire at the junk shop of Clarence Cosby (324 Brook Avenue). Nash had been off duty at home when the alarm was sounded and responded back to assist. While assisting in the placement of a hose line on the roof of the Richmond Dairy Company, Nash made a "misstep" and fell through a skylight, 30 feet to the concrete floor. He was transported to the Virginia Hospital where he later died.

### W. C. Matt
**December 21, 1916**
**Captain – Engine Company No. 7**
**14th Street & Cary Street**
**Imperial Coffee Plant**

Captain Matt, of Engine No. 7, was killed in the line of duty while operating at a fire at the Imperial Coffee Plant. Captain Matt was overcome by smoke while directing operations on the Cary Street side of the building and fell 30 feet from an extension ladder to the sidewalk below.

### J. B. Galliher
**March 13, 1921**
**Firefighter – Truck Company No. 1**
**25 W. Broad Street**
**Jurgens Store**

Firefighter Galliher, 34, of Truck No. 1, was killed in the line of duty while operating at a furniture store fire. Witnesses reported that the walls and roof of the building collapsed as a "backdraft" wrecked the building. The fire grew to 3 alarms before a "general call" was placed to request additional assistance.

### J. R. Guthrie
**March 13, 1921**
**Firefighter – Truck Company No. 1**
**25 W. Broad Street**
**Jurgens Store**

Firefighter Guthrie, 25, of Truck No. 1, was killed in the line of duty while operating at a furniture store fire. Witnesses reported that the walls and roof of the building collapsed as a "backdraft" wrecked the building. The fire grew to 3 alarms before a "general call" was placed to request additional assistance.

### G. C. Richardson
**March 13, 1921**
**Firefighter – Truck Company No. 1**
**25 W. Broad Street**
**Jurgens Store**

Firefighter Richardson, 26, of Truck No. 1, was killed in the line of duty while operating at a furniture store fire. Witnesses reported that the walls and roof of the building collapsed as a "backdraft" wrecked the building. The fire grew to 3 alarms before a "general call" was placed to request additional assistance.

### T. R. Johnson
**March 13, 1921**
**Firefighter – Truck Company No. 2**
**25 W. Broad Street**
**Jurgens Store**

Firefighter Johnson, 34, of Truck No. 2, was killed in the line of duty while operating at a furniture store fire. Witnesses reported that the walls and roof of the building collapsed as a "backdraft" wrecked the building. The fire grew to 3 alarms before a "general call" was placed to request additional assistance.

### A. N. Creasy
**October 19, 1930**
**Firefighter – Engine Company No. 1**
**25th Street & Jefferson Street**

Firefighter Creasy, of Engine No. 1, was killed when the engine that he was riding on, collided with a street car at the intersection of 25th St & Jefferson. Engine No. 1 had been responding to an alarm received from Box 161, Mechanicsville Trpk & Brauers Lane. The alarm was for a car on fire in the area.

# Line of Duty Deaths

## C. A. Cotton
**March 18, 1931**
Firefighter – Engine Company No. 13

Firefighter Cotton, 54, of Engine No. 13, was killed in the line of duty when he fell through the pole hole of Station No. 13, from the second floor to the apparatus bay. Firefighter Cotton was answering a motorcycle call when the fall occurred.

## H. C. Bottoms
**December 24, 1943**
Firefighter – Engine Company No. 8
1537 E. Main Street
Powell Brothers Store

Firefighter Bottoms, of Engine No. 8, died in the line of duty while operating at a building fire. Firefighter Bottoms was found in the alley beside the fire building by a police officer, he had died of an apparent heart attack.

## J. S. Gibson
**June 19, 1951**
Captain – Engine Company No. 14
Notts Salvage Metal Company
(No address found)

Captain Gibson, of Engine No. 14, died of an apparent heart attack while directing his company's operations at the Notts Salvage Metal Company fire.

## S. J. Wood
**January 31, 1953**
Lieutenant – Engine Company No. 9
2015 Montero Avenue

Lientenant Wood, 51, of Engine Company 9, died in the line of duty when he fell from the hose wagon while responding to a building fire.

## C. C. Jones
**December 19, 1958**
Firefighter - Engine Company No. 14
Chamberlayne Avenue & Overbrook Road

Firefighter Jones, 25, of Engine Company 14, died in the line of duty while responding to a multi-alarm fire at the Bottled Gas Corporation at 1701 Brook Road. Firefighter Jones fell off the side of the truck when it swerved to miss another vehicle.

## E. R. Bibb
**December 3, 1961**
Firefighter – Truck Company No. 3
West Broad Street, Sears and Roebuck Store

Firefighter Bibb, 48, of Truck Company 3, was killed in the line of duty when he fell from the tiller of Truck No. 3. Firefighter Bibb was teaching a trainee how to till, when the rear of the vehicle got too close to a light pole. Firefighter Bibb, let go of the railing he was holding onto to grab the wheel and the vehicle struck the light pole, sending Bibb to the sidewalk. The crash was described as "low speed."

## H. O. Hill
**March 9, 1962**
Firefighter – Truck Company No. 3
1415 Grove Avenue

Firefighter Hill, 39, of Truck No. 3, was killed in the line of duty while operating at a house fire. Firefighter Hill came down from the aerial ladder and became "sick." He was taken to the hospital where he died 1½ hours later.

## H. S. Hicks II
**June 14, 1963**
Captain – Engine Company No. 9
1001 N. 5th Street

Captain Hicks, 39, of Engine No. 9, died in the line of duty while attempting a rescue of a man in a hole. Upon Engine 9's arrival, they found a man unconscious in a hole below a condemned house. Captain Hicks donned a smoke mask and proceeded into the hole to rescue the individual when he was overcome by gas in the hole that displaced the oxygen, making his mask useless.

## D. P. Evans
**June 14, 1963**
Firefighter – Engine Company No. 9
1001 N. 5th Street

Firefighter Evans, 39, of Engine No. 9, died in the line of duty while attempting a rescue of a man in a hole. Upon Engine 9's arrival, they found a man unconscious in a hole below a condemned house. Firefighter Evans donned a smoke mask and proceeded into the hole to rescue the individual when he was overcome by gas in the hole that displaced the oxygen, making his mask useless.

## E. L. Bendle Jr.
**October 23, 1963**
Lieutenant – Engine Company No. 15
403 Ladies Mile Road

Lientenant Bendle, 42, of Engine Company 15, was killed in the line of duty while operating at a house fire. Lientenant Bendle had gone inside the house with his mask and came out to direct hose streams when he began to feel ill. He was taken to the hospital where he died of a heart attack.

## E. R. Carroll Jr.
**June 24, 1967**
Lieutenant – Training Division
Blossburg, PA

Lientenant Carroll, of the Training Division, was killed in the line

11

# LINE OF DUTY DEATHS

of duty when the plane that he was a passenger of crashed. Lientenant Carroll had been to a training school in Elmira, NY at the American LaFrance factory for aerial platform training.

## G. D. Mingee
### June 24, 1967
### Captain – Training Division
### Blossburg, PA

Captain Mingee, of the Training Division, was killed in the line of duty when the plane that he was a passenger of crashed. Captain Mingee had been to a training school in Elmira, New York, at the American LaFrance factory for aerial platform training.

## G. W. Miller
### January 21, 1970
### Firefighter – Engine Company No. 14
### 3008 1st Avenue

Firefighter Miller, of Engine Company 14, died in the line of duty while operating at an upstairs apartment fire. Firefighter Miller was the driver/operator of Engine 14 when he suffered a heart attack at the pump panel outside.

## J. W. Buckner
### August 19, 1970
### Firefighter – Engine Company No. 20
### 1201 Acorn Avenue

Firefighter Buckner, 20, of Engine Company 20, died in the line of duty while operating at a house fire. Firefighter Buckner was operating on the fire floor where he became disoriented and re-entered the fire room, collapsing behind a door. Firefighter Buckner died of carbon monoxide poisoning.

## G. Swanson
### April 12, 1972
### Firefighter – Engine Company No. 7
### 3310 Deepwater Terminal Road
### Allen Industries Warehouse

Firefighter Swanson, 29, of Engine Company 7, died in the line of duty while operating at a warehouse fire. Firefighter Swanson was killed when a bale of burlap, normally 900 pounds, had been saturated with water from fire streams and fell on top of him. Firefighter Swanson was crushed to death and four other firefighters were injured by the bale of burlap.

## J. N. Thomas
### July 2, 1973
### Lieutenant – Engine Company No. 16
### 3412 Hawthorne Avenue

Lieutenant Thomas died in the line of duty while operating at a house fire. Lieutenant Thomas laddered the porch roof and entered the attic to assist with interior operations. While descending the stairs to the 2nd floor Lieutenant Thomas suffered a heart attack and collapsed.

## G. L. Wyatt
### April 11, 1974
### Captain – Engine 10
### 2nd Street & Marshall Street

Captain Wyatt, 42, of Engine Company 10, died in the line of duty due to injuries he received as the result of an accident that occurred on April 3rd. Captain Wyatt had been riding in the officer's seat on Engine 10's wagon when it was struck by the Flying Squad aerial platform. Both units were responding to an automatic alarm at the Richmond Coliseum.

## M. Griffin
### June 19, 1997
### Firefighter – Quint Company 5

Firefighter Griffin succumbed to injuries sustained following an automobile accident he was involved in while conducting Fire Department business. Since then a memorial golf tournament has been established in his name to benefit MDA Summer Camp and the Burn Foundation.

## J. W. Hall
### January 6, 2006
### Firefighter – Quint Company 23

Firefighter Hall died in the line of duty when he suffered a heart attack on his way into work.

## B. E. Emerson Jr.
### July 27, 2006
### Lieutenant – Safety Officer

Lieutenant Emerson died in the line of duty from job related leukemia.

## B. W. Harris
### December 27, 2006
### Firefighter – Quint Company 1

Firefighter Harris died in the line of duty from job related cancer.

## P. L. Riley, Jr.
### November 30, 2007
### Procurement Officer

Lieutenant Riley died in the line of duty from job related cancer.

## The Supreme Sacrifice !

# Line of Duty Deaths

## In Memory

*Marvin Griffin*

*Jerry Hall*

*Bernard Emerson*

*Billy Harris*

*Percy L. Riley, Jr.*

# A Word From the Fire Chief

 **CITY OF RICHMOND**
**Department of Fire and Emergency Services**

201 E. Franklin Street
Richmond, VA 23219
804-646-2500

*Fire Chief*
*Robert A. Creecy*

Greetings to the Members and Friends of the Richmond Fire Department:

On October 25, 2008, the members of the City of Richmond's Department of Fire and Emergency Services recognized our 150th anniversary. While our organizational history as a municipal department began then, Richmond's fire suppression history actually started nearly fifty years before that, with citizen volunteers working together to protect the growing city from the uncontrolled ravages of fire. Therefore, it is with great pride that I now welcome you to the pages of this commemorative book which celebrates that rich history.

From the early days of volunteers with leather buckets to paid firefighters with horse drawn steam engines, to modern apparatus, our Department has always strived to become more effective and efficient in our duties. Today the Richmond Fire Department protects over 200,000 residents and the Capitol City of Virginia. While we are understandably proud of who and what we are, we need to recognize the dedication and commitment of those who came before us. In the fire service it is a time honored tradition that the senior firefighters sit down at the coffee table and mentor the newer firefighters. This tradition has continued for over 150 years, and hopefully it will continue for the next 150 years. It is my hope that the pictures and stories in this historical book will awaken memories, stimulate discussion, and allow that learning to continue.

As I said in my comments during our 150th Anniversary Banquet, we stand on the shoulders of giants. While other professions train their replacements, in the Fire Service, those who have come before embrace the tradition of developing future firefighters. To those giants of our Department who are now enjoying the rewards of retirement from full and rich careers, I thank you for your service and for your commitment to making us what we are today. To our current firefighters, I encourage you to continue serving our community and citizens to the best of your abilities. Remember each of you is writing tomorrow's history every day. Make it one of which all can be proud.

Finally, this book is the result of countless hours of work and planning by the Commemorative Book Committee, and I would be remiss if I did not thank them for their efforts and devotion to this project. Thanks also to all who contributed the information and photographs that make this book the treasure it is.

I am confident that all who take the time to peruse its pages will find themselves returning again and again to visit the photos and stories that celebrate the challenges and successes of our rich history. Please stop by this book and our stations whenever you can.

Best Regards,

 # City of Richmond
## DEPARTMENT OF FIRE AND EMERGENCY SERVICES

### MISSION
*We will provide safe and exceptional care through quality, innovative service by listening and responding to the needs of our City of Richmond family and visitors.*

### VISION
*We will be an inclusive and innovative Department that values every employee and citizen while striving to be a model organization in our community by working together to achieve excellence in every aspect of service.*

### VALUES
*We take pride in delivering quality customer service. We are committed to promptly responding with excellence through integrity and leadership.*

# CHIEFS OF RFD

### James Bosher
### 1852
(No information available)

### Lewis Bosher
### 1855
(No information available)

### John J. Fry
### 1858
The son of Hugh W. Fry, a grocer and commission merchant. Chief Fry resided on Capitol Street between 10th and 11th Streets. Appointed Chief on August 13, 1858, when the Volunteer Fire Department was organized.

### Lewis L. Barnes
### 1858-1865
Chief Barnes was appointed Chief on October 25, 1858. The Volunteer Fire Department was abolished and the Paid department began. Chief Barnes resided on 4th Street between Main and Franklin.

### Frank L. Mullen
### 1865
Chief Mullen served during the reconstruction and occupancy of the city during the Civil War by Federal Troops. He was Chief from April to May 1865.

### William A. Charters
### 1865-1870
Appointed Chief, September 22, 1865. He was Chief until being killed in the line of duty in the Capitol disaster on April 27, 1870. *(See monument on page 9)*

### George A. Ainslie
### 1870-1879
Chief Ainslie was elected Chief upon the death of Chief Charters. He was the father of Mayor George Ainslie, who was the Mayor of Richmond from 1916-1924.

### G. Watt Taylor
### 1879-1886
Chief Taylor lived at 2210 E. Broad Street and ran a grocery store at 2501 E. Broad Street.

*Chief G. W. Taylor*

### Arthur L. Fuqua
### 1886-1888
Chief Fuqua boarded at 914 E. Broad Street which was four doors down from the then Station 3. He was a Tinner by trade and served as Chief until 1888.

### W. G. Puller
### 1888-1907
Chief Puller lived at 1008 Clay Street and was a carpenter by trade. He served as Chief of the department until February 1907.

*Chief W. G. Puller*

### George C. Shaw
### 1907-1908
Chief Shaw served as Chief in Truck Company 2's quarters until his death in 1908 from injuries he suffered in a fire earlier in the day.

*Chief George C. Shaw*

### William H. Joynes
### 1908-1940
In 1938, it was believed that Chief Joynes, a painter by trade, was the oldest active Fire Chief at age 83. Chief Joynes retired in 1940 and died shortly thereafter.

*Chief William H. Joynes*

### A. F. Taylor
### 1940-1944
Chief Taylor served as Chief for most of World War II until leaving office in 1944.

*Chief A. F. Taylor*

# CHIEFS OF RFD

## John F. Finnegan Sr.
### 1944-1959

Chief Finnegan, a metal worker by trade, quickly earned the nickname "In Again Finnegan" for the way he would not allow his men to enter a burning building until he first went in and assessed the situation and determined the best

*Chief John F. Finnegan Sr.*

way to fight the fire. In one incident, Chief Finnegan was hit in the head hard enough to dent his metal helmet. Escorted out of the structure by his son he glanced at his helmet and was quoted as saying "Well how about that" and he turned and went back in to help his men. Chief Finnegan died in office January 29, 1959 less than two months from mandatory retirement age.

## Edgar A. Sherry
### 1959-1971

Chief Sherry was a former Fire Bureau Drillmaster and Administrative Assistant Chief. Chief Sherry was the first Richmond Fire Chief to be appointed as a direct result of a promotional exam. He died in office of a heart attack on November 6, 1971.

*Chief Edgar A. Sherry*

## John F. Finnegan Jr.
### 1972-1978

Chief Finnegan rose quickly through the ranks of the Fire Bureau and was often quoted as saying "between the ages of 6 and 21, I went to more second alarm fires than most firemen have been to by the time they were 40". He was appointed chief on July 22, 1972, retiring from office on January 7, 1978.

*Chief John F. Finnegan Jr.*

## Ronald C. Lewis
### 1978-1995

Chief Lewis was appointed Chief on November 16, 1978 after retiring from the Philadelphia, Pennsylvania Fire Department where he had attained the rank of Battalion Chief. Chief Lewis was the first African American, and outsider, to be named as Richmond's Fire Chief. Under Chief Lewis' command, a 60-hour work week dropped to 56 hours, modern equipment replaced old apparatus, and firefighters received new uniforms. Chief Lewis headed a department of 510 employees and protected 62.5 square miles. Also under his leadership, a highly skilled dive team was developed, a hazardous materials unit was created and the Fire Information Management System, which computerized all information in the department, was installed. Chief Lewis retired in 1995.

*Chief Ronald C. Lewis*

## Jack K. McElfish
### 1995-2003

Chief McElfish was appointed chief on December 18, 1995. He had been the fire chief of Wallingford, Connecticutt, and most recently as chief of Clayton County, Georgia. Chief McElfish brought the "Total Quint Con-

*Chief Jack K. McElfish*

cept" to the Richmond Fire Department by combining engine and truck companies replacing them with a Quint apparatus in each of Richmond's twenty firehouses. Chief McElfish retired from office on October 12, 2002 and returned to Georgia to become Chief of the Gwinnett County Fire Department.

## CHIEFS OF RFD

### Larry R. Tunstall
### 2003-2005

Larry R. Tunstall, a 34-year veteran, was the first African American to serve as Chief of Operations/Administration. Hired as a firefighter on September 29, 1969, he was promoted to Lieutenant in February 1976, to Captain in May of 1979, Deputy Battalion Chief in 1984, to Battalion Chief in 1987, to Division Chief on June 10, 1998, and Fire Marshal Chief on August 26, 2002. On September 12, 2003, he was appointed Chief/Director of Fire and Emergency Services. Larry R. Tunstall is the first African American to come through the ranks to the top position. He resigned from office in 2005.

*Chief Larry R. Tunstall*

### Robert A. Creecy
### 2005-Present

Hired as a firefighter on June 8, 1982, Robert Creecy, rose through the ranks of the department. On May 2, 2005, Battalion Chief Creecy was tapped to be the Interim Fire Chief by Mayor L. Douglas Wilder and appointed into the permanent position on July 8th. He commands a department of 432 sworn firefighters and twelve support staff, with a budget of $39 million, and calls for service approaching 29,000 per year. Fire Chief Creecy currently serves as Richmond's 20th chief of the Department.

*Chief Robert A. Creecy*

*Richmond Burning, Civil War Era*

 # Richmond Fire Department History

In 1679, Captain William Byrd inherited a large amount of land near the falls of the James River. On this land, he established Fort Charles with fifty men to provide protection to the area. His son, Colonel William Byrd, expanded on his father's beginnings and built a large business in farming, manufacturing, mining, and trading. Scottish workers for Colonel Byrd's businesses lived in an area that became known as "Rocketts". In 1737, Colonel Byrd had Major William Mayo lay out a town to be called "Richmond". The area, from what is now 17th Street to 25th Street and from Broad Street to Cary Street, covered thirty two blocks with each block divided into four lots. Several lots were set aside for churches and other public buildings.

One of the first recorded fire prevention efforts in Richmond was a 1741 Virginia Assembly Act. This act prohibited "the building in the town of wooden chimneys, and commanded that within the space of three years all existing wooden chimneys should be replaced with brick, or pulled down…"

In 1742, Richmond was officially incorporated as a town. The first large fire in the new town of Richmond occurred in 1781 during the Revolutionary War. While most of the men were away in the army, Benedict Arnold advanced into Richmond with 800 red-coated British soldiers and sailors, setting fires to destroy revolutionary supplies and facilities. While these fires caused significant damage to Richmond, they did not change the outcome of the war.

The successful outcome of the Revolutionary War created a strong nationalism movement in the newly formed United States of America. Each state formalized its boundaries and established their state capitol for their new seats of government. Richmond only consisted of about three hundred homes, but it was selected as Virginia's Capitol and incorporated as a city in 1782. In addition to selecting Richmond as the State Capitol, the Virginia Assembly ordered that a new capitol building be built.

In 1785, the Friendship Fire Company was formed. This volunteer organization was created to prevent accidental fires in the City of Richmond. While this organization was initially involved in prevention efforts only, at some unknown point they acquired suppression equipment and began to fight fires as a volunteer fire company.

Richmond's second big fire occurred in 1787 when Mrs. Harthorne's frame home caught on fire. The blaze spread rapidly and in three hours, destroying 40 to 50 buildings in the city. The citizens of the city fought valiantly, but bucket brigades and wells were not enough stop the fire. It was only when two homes in the path of the fire were destroyed to create a fire stop that the flames were finally extinguished.

In 1794, an emigrant brought fire insurance to Richmond and the United States. The nation's first fire insurance policy was written on the Masonic Hall in Richmond by the Mutual Assurance Society in that same year. This policy was still in effect in the 1970's. The Mutual Assurance Society was soon copied and a number of additional fire insurance companies were established. These companies played a significant role in early fire prevention efforts by refusing to insure buildings that did not follow established guidelines in building materials and construction.

Richmond's next major fire is still listed as one of the worst fires in the United States. On December 26, 1811, a packed audience was attending the final performance of a play in the Richmond Theatre. This special event

# Richmond Fire Department History

featured the main performance, followed by a special religious play or Pantomine. The second play was called "The Bleeding Nun or Agnes and Raymond." Records indicate that 518 adult tickets and 80 children tickets had been sold. There were also an estimated 50 people in the galleries. The Pantomime began right after the main play finished. During the first act, a chandelier hanging from the ceiling illuminated the stage. Once the curtain fell, the chandelier was raised back towards the ceiling to prepare for the second act. After the chandelier had been raised, it was discovered that the lamp had not yet been extinguished. The stage manager attempted to lower the chandelier back down to extinguish the lamp, but the cords became tangled and the chandelier got stuck. The stage manager's efforts to free the chandelier started it swinging in place and it came into contact with a stage scene. There were 35 scenes and once the first one caught on fire, it rapidly spread to all of them. The Richmond Theatre had a very basic roof of pine planks nailed over rafters and covered in shingles. There was no plaster protecting the rafters which were only 6 or 7 feet above the top of the scenes. Once the scenes were burning, it very quickly spread to the entire ceiling of the theatre. With the fire running along the ceiling of the building, the audience was quickly blanketed in hot gases and thick heavy smoke.

While the fire was disastrous enough, egress from the theatre was actually worse. The building only had one entrance for the entire audience. To escape the fire, patrons in the upper and lower boxes either had to go down a narrow angular staircase in thick choking smoke or jump out of the windows. Initially the fire was not noticed by the audience since it was behind the curtains. Once the cry of "fire" went out and the fire was seen, the crowd panicked and a number of people were crushed. Seventy-two people lost their lives including the Governor of Virginia and a number of prominent local officials.

This disaster encouraged the citizens of Richmond to examine fire suppression efforts in the city. By the end of 1812, there were apparently several volunteer fire organizations operating throughout the city. An 1812 Richmond newspaper article talks about a Shockoe Hill fire company selling its engine at auction. Another news article in 1815 talks about Richmond having an engine and a horse drawn hook and ladder truck. While equipment was improving in the city, water supply continued to be problematic. It was largely dependent on private wells and springs, as well as the periodic public wells located on street corners. This lack of a dedicated and readily available water supply became very apparent after a fire on Main Street in 1815. The fire destroyed five houses after it took 40 minutes to form a bucket line long enough to reach the nearest water supply.

Concerned about the Main Street fire, the Capital, Rocketts, and Shockoe Hill Volunteer Fire Companies came together in April of 1816 and formed the Richmond Fire Society. This organization was created "for the purpose of rendering mutual assistance in the hour of peril, and to extend the influence of effective friendship. Each member was required to pay dues, to buy a $.75 cent book of regulation, and to provide on their own two buckets, two bags, and a bed socket-key" (to unbolt and remove heavy bed frames from burning homes). A newspaper article said that members were also required to purchase "a stiff hat painted blue, with the name his company in a semicircle in front, and his own name and the number of his company in back." Membership was limited to no more than 36 members. In the event of a fire, the owner of the property was in charge of firefighting operations. If the owner was not present, the president of the society assumed command. The secretary was the only paid officer of the organization and received $15.00 a year. Fines of $2.00 were imposed for missing fires, and a fine of $1.00 was imposed for missing a regular equipment inspection. Discipline issues were also addressed by fines and it was not uncommon for the secretary to be fined more than his yearly salary. These companies were often made up of the sons of prominent Richmond families and each company had their own side brake engines, reels, and hoses. They also sent representatives to the annual Richmond Fire Department meetings.

The first hand-pumped engines in Richmond were apparently used at a fire at the penitentiary in 1823. The improved equipment did not save the building, but kept the fire in check long enough for the walls to be broken down so all of the prisoners could be released.

In 1830, the City of Richmond began to work seriously on improving fire safety efforts. Money was budgeted for a water supply system, a reservoir, water-powered pump-house, and private hydrants for the community. This new system proved extremely valuable for fire suppression efforts in Richmond. With the new water supply system in place, the fire department purchased a Hydraulian. This powerful engine was pumped by forty men and it could throw a stream of water over the State Capital. Unfortunately, it was so heavy it was difficult to move, so a small building was built for it near the water basin. When a fire occurred, the Hydraulian would be put into service to pump water as far as the hoses would reach.

In 1837 to increase fire protection in the city, council turned over control of the fire department to the Richmond Fire Association, an insurance company made up mostly of firefighters. The Richmond Fire Association would control the fire department from 1837 until 1855. During this time, they added new engines, doubled the water supply, and standardized alarms. Under the Richmond Fire Association, the city was divided into wards. No 1, Jefferson Ward covered all areas east of 15th Street. No 2, Madison Ward covered all areas west of 15th Street and east of 7th Street. No 3, Monroe Ward, included everything west of 7th Street. When a fire was spotted that ward's bell tower would ring one, two, or three times depending on the ward's number. It would then ring quickly until the bell towers from the other wards began to ring. Once the other towers were ringing, it would continue to toll its ward number until the fire was extinguished. The other wards' bells would ring normally after the initial alarm with periodic stops to ring the ward number where the fire was located. This system continued until 1870 when the electric fire-alarm system was introduced.

In 1844, a city landmark located at 12th and Main caught fire. While not much is known about the actual blaze, there was much discussion about the building's great height. The building was considered remarkable because it was four stories high.

By 1853, fire suppression within the City of Richmond was provided by at least eight volunteer fire companies. These included Capital, Rocketts, Shockoe Hill, Phoenix, and Friendship Fire Companies. After a large fire destroyed the Virginia Woolen Mills and damaged the Haxall Mills in that same year, city council realized that Richmond's fire equipment was inadequate to protect the city. They ordered the purchase of four modern hand-engines, several hook and ladders, and a large supply of new hose.

A May 15, 1854 report says the purchased hook and ladders contains: 5 ladders; 8 hooks; 4 lanterns and holders; 2 axes; 2 picks; 1 crow bar; 2 wrenches; and 1 drag rope/side rope. The cost of each truck was $650.00.

Because it was made up of volunteers, the Richmond Fire Department was very much a social organization. One of the highlights of the volunteers was their semi-annual "washings" which were days of great fun in competition, games, and eating. This same spirit of fun continued when the first of the new engines arrived. The Phoenix Fire Company met their new Engine 3 at the wharf with a band and escorted it throughout the city streets to its new home with honor.

In 1855, the Penitentiary caught fire again. While the volunteer fire companies worked with citizens and the military to rescue the prisoners and extinguish the fire, the city council was not totally happy with the efforts of the Fire Department. They tried to organize it under John J. Fry, its head engineer, and made it report to a city council committee. This did not change the young men who sang and cheered on their ways to fires, and who were so competitive that they were sometimes unjustly accused of starting fires just so they could be the first one to arrive on scene.

On October 25, 1858, the city council passed an ordinance disbanding the volunteer companies and establishing a paid fire brigade. The new brigade consisted of Engines 1, 2, 3, 4, and Trucks 1 and 2. Lewis L. Barnes was appointed Fire Chief. The brigade consisted of a total of twelve full time men and paid on-call hosemen and laddermen. While the department's initial equipment consisted of hand-pumped engines, it was also at this time that they began replacing hand-pumped engines with steam engines.

In 1860, Ettinger and Edmunds of Richmond built a steam engine for the Russian government. It amazed crowds when it threw water over the American Hotel located on 12th and Main Streets. The Richmond Fire Department placed an order with Ettinger and Edmunds for its own steam engine that same year.

In 1861 Richmond became the capital of the Confederate States of America. The city itself was an important logistical and manufacturing site during the war. In April of 1865 after Confederate forces were unable to hold city from advancing Union forces, they were

*Damage to Richmond Following the Civil War*

# Richmond Fire Department History

forced to retreat from Richmond. To keep supplies from falling into enemy hands, Confederate troops set fire to Shockoe Warehouse, Dibrell's Warehouse, Mayo's Warehouse, and the Mayo Bridge. Confederate sympathizers and looters set their own fires or used the warehouse fires as an opportunity to loot and destroy additional buildings. A strong wind which began during the evacuation also helped spread fire throughout the city. When the fire department responded and attempted to extinguish the fires, Confederate sympathizers cut their hoses and threatened them. Hotels, buildings, banks, a church, and many of the Confederate government's buildings, including the State Armory, the Navy Yards, and the War Department, were destroyed in addition to the warehouses. It was only when Union forces entered the city and assisted local officials with dynamiting several buildings to stop the spread of the fire, that the fires were finally extinguished. The fires destroyed both sides of Main Street all the way to the river between 8th Street and 15th Street, and from 20th Street to 23rd Street. Only two buildings remained standing in the entire area, the Post Office and a bank building. In addition to the loss of the center of the city, twelve inmates at the Poor House were killed during an explosion at the same time. It would take five years and a legal battle before martial law was abolished and the city was once again in civilian control.

*Richmond Fire Department in 1893*

By 1870, Richmond was back to normal and under civilian control again. It was in this year that whiskey owners sought retribution from losses sustained when city officials destroyed whiskey inventories to keep it out of the hands of looters during the evacuation fires. Through legal action, whiskey owners seized possession of the fire department's apparatus. Concerned citizens raised $17,000, temporarily appeasing whiskey owners to return the apparatus to the fire department. The city later settled the remaining debt with the whiskey owners.

An 1870 report shows the fire department had 90 runs, 88 men, 15 fire boxes, and 1 inspector. There were 48 flue fires with less than $10 damage and 27 fires that exceeded $10. The biggest fire of that year (and one of the biggest in the city) occurred on Christmas Day 1870. Shortly after 1 a.m. on December 25 a fire was discovered by the night watchman at the Spotswood Hotel, located on the corner of Eighth and Main Streets. The historic old hotel had 200 guests registered, eight of them perished in the fire. The flames, aided with a strong wind, destroyed the all wooden hotel as well as five nearby businesses.

In 1880, each fire company in the city consisted of a full-time engineer, driver, and reel operator. Each company also had runners, or call men, who lived in various parts of the city and were expected to respond to fire calls. The runners were paid a stipend and had 30 minutes to respond to a fire. Unfortunately, because their transportation usually consisted of running to the scene, they often arrived after the fire had already been extinguished.

# Richmond Fire Department History

In 1881, the International Fire Chiefs Association (IAFC) had a membership of 126. Richmond Fire Chief G. Watt Taylor, a charter member, hosted the ninth conference in Richmond (the 51st conference was also held in Richmond in 1923). Issues discussed at the conference included: probationary terms for new firefighters, building construction issues, and recommendations that elevator shafts be constructed of brick or concrete.

In 1884, Truck Company House 2 was built at 1805 East Grace Street. Truck 2 was the only Richmond truck company ever housed in a single company fire house. They remained in service at that location until 1952 when the station was closed and the company was moved to Engine House 2.

In 1888, several significant events occurred in Richmond. The fire department was placed in the hands of a board of fire commissioners. Another major event occurred on February 2. The Richmond Union Passenger Railway, the first practical electric trolley in the United States, began regular operations in the city with 10 streetcars. For the first time, workers did not have to live downtown to get to work every day. Soon residential neighborhoods were being built to the north and west of the city as more people used public transportation to come to work.

An 1894 *Richmond News Leader* reported Engine Company 1 responded to 25 runs and working 26½ hours at fires. The article also reported annual salaries with the captain at call earning $300, the permanent engineer making $960, the hostler and helper each earning $840, and each hoseman at call made $240.

By 1900, the 23 men of the Richmond Fire Department earned $55 a month. There were eight steam engines and several horse-drawn hook-and-ladder trucks in the city. The department was responding to 330 alarms in a year with an annual budget of $68,530. Chief Puller, the fire chief, was unhappy with the continued use of call men. "Five of our companies still have to depend on call hosemen and laddermen. ... Richmond should have a stationed or permanent force in her fire department and not have to depend on men working in all parts of the city to protect the lives and property of her citizens from fire," he said. It was 12 more years before the chief's vision was realized with every firefighter becoming a full time employee in 1912. The full time firefighters worked 24 hours a day with one day off a week.

On March 29, 1901, defective wiring started a fire at the Jefferson Hotel. The initial alarm was received from Box 723 and within a short time every firefighter

*Franklin Street in 1905*

*Cary Street in 1911*

*Chamber of Commerce in 1910*

23

# Richmond Fire Department History

*Broad Street in 1914*

*14th Street Bridge in 1917*

*Broad Street in 1927*

in the city was on scene. There were no lives lost, but the hotel had significant damage.

During the early 1900's, the Richmond Fire Department saw significant growth as new fire companies were placed into service as the city continued to grow. Companies placed into service were: Engine 9 (1902), Engine 10 (1905), Engines 11 and 12 (1908), and Truck 4 (1909).

In 1910, the small independent City of Manchester agreed to a political consolidation with the much larger city of Richmond. Two of the key points in this decision were Richmond's agreement to build a "free bridge" across the James River, and the agreement that a courthouse would remain in Manchester and be maintained indefinitely. To provide fire protection to this new area, Engine 13 was established in 1910, followed by Truck 5 in 1913, and Engine 17 in 1915.

The first motorized fire equipment was placed in service at Engine Company 4, located at 207 North 3rd Street in 1911. "One motorized engine did the work of five horses, one engine, and one combination vehicle". These engines were also cheaper to maintain at just $267 for a six-month period, while horses cost $1,538 for the same time period. Chief Puller pushed for more motorized vehicles arguing that even delivery wagons were motorized while the fire department continued to use horse-drawn equipment. In 1912, the department purchased three chief cars, another motorized engine, and a motorized aerial ladder. A newspaper article reported that on October 7, 1930, the last horse-drawn apparatus in the city, located at Engine Company 11, was taken out of service and sold.

The Richmond Fire Department eliminated call men in 1912 with all full time firefighters working 24 hours a day with one day off a week. This new system had its share of problems with low pay, a significant reason 24 men resigned the first year, many to take better paying jobs.

In 1914, the City of Richmond annexed a large section of what is now northside, acquiring the growing communities of Ginter Park, Barton Heights, and Highland Park to name a few. Each of these small towns had their own fire department, though only Ginter Park had any real equipment. To serve these new areas, the fire department placed Engines 14, 15, and 16 into service.

In 1918, the Board of Commissioners, which had controlled the fire department for 30 years, was abolished and the fire depart-

# Richmond Fire Department History

*Engine 11, Last RFD Steamer Sold*

ment was placed under the control of an administrative board. Less than a year later (1919), the fire department was put under the jurisdiction of the Department of Public Safety. The fire alarm department was also placed under the Department of Public Safety in this year. In 1920, a fire prevention bureau was organized and placed under the direction of Assistant Chief L. S. Jones.

On March 13, 1921 at 12:35 p.m., a fire was discovered on the third floor of the Hopkin's Furniture Store, located at 25-27-29 West Broad Street. A second alarm was sounded at 12:37 p.m., a third alarm at 12:40 p.m., and a general call (6-6-6) for the entire department at 12:45 p.m. As thousands watched the fire from the streets, a backdraft caused an explosion, collapsing the walls of the building. Firefighters J. B. Galliher, J. R. Guthrie, and G. C. Richardson of Truck Company 1, T. R. Johnston from Truck Company 2, and Adolph Heinecke, a citizen volunteer helping the firefighters, were killed. Several other fire companies had close calls including Captain Meadors and his crew from Engine Company 1. They had been on the roof of the building just minutes before the explosion. They had been unable to get the needed pressure from their lines and were on the ground changing hydrants when the walls collapsed. This was the single largest loss of life for the Richmond Fire Department.

During the 1920's, the fire department purchased a large amount of new equipment. A Seagrave Water Tower (currently stationed at Station 20) was purchased in 1922 for $22,500. The mast on the solid rubber-wheeled tower extended 65 feet high and could deliver more than 1,128 gallons a minute. It remained in service until 1950, fighting its last big fire at the Monument Methodist Church, located at Allen and Park Avenues. The 1920's also saw a number of new hook and ladder trucks for the city, search lights, soda, acid, and foamite extinguishers, triple combination motorized pumping engines, and steam engines with 1000 gallon capacity pumpers. By the end of the 1920's, however, steam engines were no longer desired apparatus and were slowly phased out of service. The department's inventory list for 1928 shows two steam engines in reserve. One year later in 1929, no steam engines are listed in the City of Richmond.

On November 17, 1921, a second shift was added to the fire department. This changed personnel from working six days a week with one day off, to working 24 hours on and 24 hours off.

On February 8, 1922, at 4:34 a.m., a fire alarm was received from Box 34, located at 13th and Cary Streets. This building, the Lexington Hotel, was reported to be a raging inferno when the first apparatus arrived on scene. The fire traveled throughout the building, rapidly using the open elevator shaft to quickly consume floor after floor of the building. A second alarm was sounded four minutes later. Shortly after that, a general alarm (6-6-6) was sounded, bringing every piece of equipment in the city, except two reserve companies. Those two companies responded at 5:20 a.m. and 5:24 a.m., leaving only three obsolete engines and two truck companies in the entire city. Numerous hotel guests awoke to find themselves trapped in their rooms. They jumped out of windows or fell from window ledges, trying to escape the flames. Twelve people died and five additional buildings burned before the fire was finally extinguished.

# Richmond Fire Department History

*Pump Ops*

*House Fire*

*House Fire*

# Richmond Fire Department History

On July 1, 1972, the department eliminated the department's last hose wagons. The Richmond Fire Departments final five hose wagons had been in service with Engine Companies 2, 5, 12, 17, and 18. These companies were reduced to 15 members, eliminating 15 additional positions.

In 1974, the Richmond Fire Bureau ended its annual fire safety and fireworks show after twenty-five years. These shows were extremely popular with the community but had become increasingly more expensive. When new construction near the stadium forced the cancelation of the annual show, the decision was made to bring the tradition to a close.

*Chief Finnegan, Jr.*

In the early morning hours of June 26, 1975, two Little Oil Company gasoline storage tanks ignited in Richmond's southside. Firefighters, reinforced with foam equipment from the United States Air Force and Navy, were finally able to extinguish the blaze 19 hours later.

On July 1, 1975, the City of Richmond received a Class II rating from the Insurance Service Office, a national organization that evaluates the firefighting abilities of cities. The ranking was the highest available since no city at that time have ever received a Class I rating.

On November 16, 1978, Ronald C. Lewis was appointed to the position of fire chief. Chief Lewis came to Richmond after retiring as a battalion chief with the Philadelphia Fire Department. Chief Lewis was the first person hired from outside the department, as well as the first African-American to be appointed to the position of fire chief.

In November 1979, Firefighter Barbara Hicks was hired as the city's first female firefighter. Firefighter Spring (married name) retired from the fire department in 2005 after twenty five years of dedicated service.

During the 1980's and 90's, the fire department worked on improving the service provided to citizens. The department made an effort to expand its fire safety and prevention efforts by going out into the community. The department faced difficult budgetary decisions during this period with numerous personnel positions and fire companies eliminated. *(See the station section of this book for more information about fire company reductions.)*

In addition to fire companies, other command and support positions were eliminated, including Division Chief of Training on April 1, 1992, and North and South Divisions and Battalion 4 on October 1, 1995.

In November of 1990, the Richmond Fire Department added a first responder program to assist the ambulance service with medical calls. This new service dramatically increased the department's call volume with emergency medical calls quickly becoming a significant number of our responses.

On September 17, 1996, Engine 14 and Truck 6 were combined to create Quint Company 14. This was the first Quint in the City of Richmond.

On January 1, 1997, three rescue companies were placed into service in the City of Richmond. Rescue 1 assumed the duties of the water rescue team. Rescue 2 became the confined space/high angle team. Rescue 3 assumed the duties of the Hazmat Team.

On May 1, 1997, thirty-one new Pierce Fire Trucks were ordered from Singer Associates under the new Total Quint Concept. Quints have the ability to perform five functions: water tank, pump, hoses, ground ladders, and aerial ladders. These trucks included: 14 75-foot

*Baseball Team*

# Richmond Fire Department History

*Fully-Involved House Fire*

*I-64 Car Fire*

*Tyrone Street, 2008*

*I-95 MVA*

*35th Street House Fire, September 2008*

*915 N. 25th Street*

# Richmond Fire Department History

*28th Street MVA with Entrapment*

*Semmes Avenue House Fire*

Quints, 4 105-foot Quints, 1 100-foot platform Quint, 9 Quick Response Vehicles (QRV), and 3 rescue trucks. The trucks were built and placed into service over a two-year period. On November 20, 1997, the first two trucks, Rescue 1 and Rescue 2, went into service. On December 1, 1998, the last truck, Quint 18, went into service. On August 20, 1998, Truck Company 7, the City of Richmond's last ladder company, went out of service at 0930 hours.

In November 2003, the Richmond Fire Department Headquarters moved from 501 North 9th Street to 550 East Marshall Street. This new location was the old Blues Armory, and had previously housed Engine Company 3 and Fire Headquarters. Fire headquarters remained at this location until August 2008 when they moved into their current location at 201 East Franklin Street.

On March 26, 2004, the Richmond Fire Department received a 911 call reporting a building fire at 933 West Broad Street. This was a construction site of a four story apartment building being built to house Virginia Commonwealth University students. The unprotected building burned quickly and strong wind gusts helped spread the fire to nearby businesses and homes. By the time the fire was finally extinguished, 26 buildings and 22 vehicles had been damaged or destroyed by the fast moving fire, but no lives were lost.

On October 25, 2008, 150 years to the day after city council passed an ordinance establishing a paid fire department, over 550 people attended a banquet at the Richmond Marriott. The event was well attended by firefighters, their families, retirees, and local officials gathering to remember and celebrate the proud history of the Richmond Fire Department.

*Surround and Drown!*

# Apparatus Through The Years

## 1865

*Engine 3 Following the Burning of Richmond During the Civil War*

## Apparatus Through The Years

### 1859

*Cowing & Company Hand Pumper*

### 1915

*Mack AB Hose Wagon*

### 1920

*Bulldog Mack*

*Indian Motorcycle Ad*

### 1922

*Big Chief Indian Motorcycle*

33

# Apparatus Through The Years

1929

*GMC Hose and Chemical Wagon*

1931

*GMC-American LaFrance Hose Wagon*

1938

*GMC Hose Wagon*

1945

*Mack 19 LS Aerial*

# Apparatus Through The Years

## 1951

Mack 45A

## 1952

Oren Hose Wagon

## 1956

Mack B85

## 1961

Mack Tractor

35

# Apparatus Through The Years

## 1962

*Mack C95F*

## 1966

*Oren Foam Pumper*

## 1969

*Oren 100' Aerial*

# Apparatus Through The Years

## 1970

*Maxim Pumper*

## 1977

*Seagrave Aerial Ladder*

## 1978

*American LaFrance Engine*

## 1990

*Kovatch Pumper*

37

# Apparatus Through The Years

## 1992

*Seagrave Pumpers*

### Quint Aerial Units

Pictured is one of fourteen 75′ Pierce Heavy Duty Aerial units delivered to Chief Jack K. McElfish and the Richmond Fire Department during 1998. This model featured a 500 gallon tank, a 75′ all-steel 3 section aerial ladder, 2000 GPM Hale fire pump, 20 gallon class A foam cell, and a Pierce Dash chassis with seating for up to six firefighters. Also delivered was a 100′ Platform model and four 105′ aerial models. These units were added to Richmond's first Quint, a 75′ Ferrara HME, completing the Total Quint Concept encompassing all 20 fire stations.

## 1998

*Pierce Quint 75′ Aerial*

# Richmond Fire Department
# Fire Stations

*Remembering the 343*

# Engine House 1

*Engine House 1 at 25th near Broad*

*Built in 1910, Engine House 1 at 306 N. 25th Street*

*Engine Company 1*

40

# ENGINE HOUSE 1

*Current Fire Station 1 located at 308 N. 24th Street*

Engine Company 1 began as Richmond, Virginia's 1st career fire house. It's service began on October 25, 1858, housed at 306 N. 25th Street. In 1911, the ever-evolving Engine Company 1, along with Engine Company 4, became one of the first motorized fire companies in the city. The company was relocated, along with Truck 2, in April of 1962 to new quarters at 308 N. 24th Street where it remains today. On February 19, 1998, Engine Company 1 & Truck Company 2 combined to form Quint Company 1 with a new Quint apparatus added into service. Today Fire Station 1 is home to Quint Company 1, Rescue Company 1, and Battalion Chief 1.

*Engine House 1, 1910*

*1978 American LaFrance*

*Quint Company 1*

*Quint 1, a 1998 Pierce Rear Mount Aerial*

# Engine House 2

Steamer 2

Steamer 2

Engine 2, a 1922 Seagrave

Engine Company 2 commenced service on October 25, 1858, housed at 2025 E. Main Street. In 1899, Engine Company 2 moved to new quarters at 2016 E. Main Street, where it served for the next 63 years. In April 1962, the company moved one final time to share quarters at 308 N. 24th Street with Engine Company 1. Engine Company 2 was disbanded on January 1, 1973 after 115 years of proud service to the community.

Wagon 2, a 1952 Oren

Engine House 2 at 2016 E. Main Street in 1942

42

# Truck House 2

Truck Company 2 began service on October 25, 1858 at the corner of 18th and East Graceland Streets. In 1884, they moved into new quarters at 1805 East Grace Street. It was from this location they served as the only Richmond truck company ever assigned to a single company house. Truck House 2 was closed in 1952, and the company was relocated into Engine House 2 at 2016 East Main Street. In April of 1962, Truck Company 2 was relocated to Engine House 1 at 308 North 24th Street. The company was disbanded after 140 years of service on February 19, 1998. Personnel from Engine 1 and Truck 2 combined to form Quint Company 1, which continues to serve the City of Richmond to this day.

*Hook and Ladder Company 2*

*Hook and Ladder 2*

*Truck 4 at Truck House 2*

*Hook and Ladder Company 2*

43

# Engine House 3 & Truck 1

*Engine House 3 and Fire Headquarters in 1895 Located at 908 E. Broad Street*

*Engine House 3 at 723 East Leigh Street*

**B**eginning service on October 25, 1858, Engine Company 3 was initially housed at 906 E. Broad Street with Truck Company 1. Both companies moved into new quarters at 908 E. Broad Street in 1895. On March 20, 1966, both companies were again relocated to a newly constructed Fire Station 3 at 723 East Leigh Street. Making room for the Coliseum to be built, Fire Station 3 was torn down in 1968, and Engine Company 3 and Truck Company 1 were relocated to 411 N. 6th Street at the old Richmond Armory building. Engine Company 3 was disbanded on July 1, 1981, after 123 years of proud service to the citizens of Richmond.

*Engine House 3 at 411 N. 6th Street and 1979 100' Calavar Firebird*

*1920's Seagrave Wooden Aerial Truck 1*

44

# Engine House 3 & Truck 1

Truck Company 1 was placed in service on October 25, 1858, and was housed at 906 East Broad Street with Engine Company 3. In 1895, the truck company and engine company moved to new quarters just one door down at 908 East Broad Street. On March 20, 1966, both companies again relocated, this time to a newly constructed Fire Station 3 located at 723 East Leigh Street. Two years later in 1968, both companies were relocated to 411 North 6th Street, the old Richmond Armory, so Fire Station 3 could be demolished to make room for the new Richmond Coliseum. In April of 1981, the company parted ways with Engine Company 3, joining Engine Company 5 at 324 West Leigh Street. Engine Company 5 and Truck Company 1 were combined on January 6, 1998, forming Quint Company 5 which serves to this day.

Horse-Drawn Wagon 3

1939 Chevrolet Rescue Wagon 1

Truck 1, a 1967 Oren with a 1957 Pirsch Aerial

1964 Oren Engine 3

1920 American LaFrance Hook and Ladder 1

45

# Engine House 3 & Truck 1

*Engine Company 3*

*Hook and Ladder Company 1*

*Hook and Ladder 1*

*Engine Company 3*

46

# ENGINE HOUSE 4

Engine Company 4 was placed into service on October 25, 1858, the day the Richmond Fire Department was established. The engine company was housed at 207 North 3rd Street. In 1911, Engine Company 4, along with Engine Company 1, became the first motorized fire companies in the City of Richmond. In 1952, the company was relocated to 200 South Laurel Street with Engine Company 6. They moved one last time in April of 1966 to 2223 West Cary Street with Engine 12. Engine Company 4 served from this location until they were disbanded on July 1, 1972 after 114 years of service.

*Engine Company 4*

*Horse Drawn Wagon 4*

*1911 Knox Pumper*
*First Motorized Apparatus in the Richmond Fire Department*

*Engine House 4 at 207 N. 3rd Street*

47

# Engine House 5

Engine Company House 5 was originally placed in service in 1849 as a volunteer fire and police station at 200 W. Marshall Street. In 1862, paid staff of the Richmond Fire Department took over operations at Steamer House 5 making it a career fire house. In 1968, Engine Company 5 moved to new quarters at 324 W. Leigh Street along with Truck Company 1. On January 6, 1998, Engine Company 5 and Truck Company 1 were combined to form Quint Company 5. Serving as one of Richmond's busiest fire stations, Quint Company 5 remains housed at 324 W. Leigh Street to this day.

*Newly Built Engine House 5 at 324 W. Leigh Street*

*Present Day Station 5*

*Steamer House 5*
*Brook and Marshall in the Late 1800s*

# ENGINE HOUSE 5

*Steamer 5, circa 1890*

*Anslie Carriage Wagon 5*

*1930 American LaFrance Wagon 5*

*Engine 5, a 1953 Mack*

*Aerial Platform 1, a 1967 American LaFrance Aero chief*

*1992 Seagrave*

*Quint 5, a 1998 Pierce Rear Mount Tower Ladder*

*Current Quint 5, a 2006 Mid-mount tower Ladder*

49

# Engine House 5

*Engine 5 A-Shift*

*Quint 5 A-Shift*

*Engine 5 B-Shift*

*Quint 5 B-Shift*

*Engine 5 C-Shift*

*Quint 5 C-Shift*

*1980's Station 5*

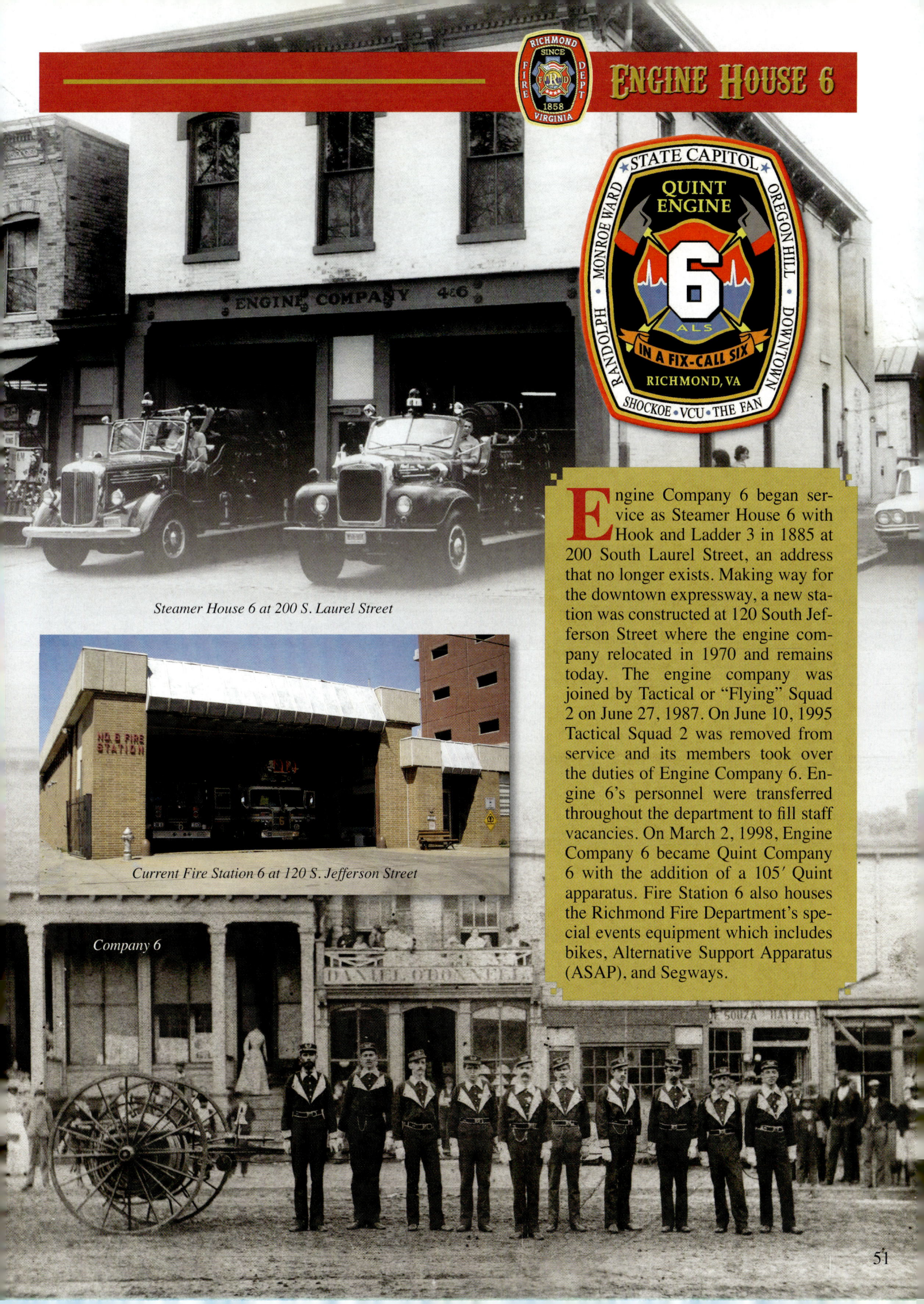

# ENGINE HOUSE 6

*Steamer House 6 at 200 S. Laurel Street*

*Current Fire Station 6 at 120 S. Jefferson Street*

*Company 6*

Engine Company 6 began service as Steamer House 6 with Hook and Ladder 3 in 1885 at 200 South Laurel Street, an address that no longer exists. Making way for the downtown expressway, a new station was constructed at 120 South Jefferson Street where the engine company relocated in 1970 and remains today. The engine company was joined by Tactical or "Flying" Squad 2 on June 27, 1987. On June 10, 1995 Tactical Squad 2 was removed from service and its members took over the duties of Engine Company 6. Engine 6's personnel were transferred throughout the department to fill staff vacancies. On March 2, 1998, Engine Company 6 became Quint Company 6 with the addition of a 105' Quint apparatus. Fire Station 6 also houses the Richmond Fire Department's special events equipment which includes bikes, Alternative Support Apparatus (ASAP), and Segways.

51

# Engine House 6

ALS Quint 6 C-Shift

Engine 6 A-Shift

Engine 6 C-Shift

ALS Quint 6 A-Shift

ALS Quint 6 B-Shift

52

# ENGINE HOUSE 6

*Horse-drawn Engine 6*

*Hose Wagon 6, a 1916 Mack AB*

*Engine 6, a 1920 Ahrens Fox Pumper*

*1958 Mack*

*1977 American LaFrance*

*Engine 6, a 1992 Seagrave*

*Attack 6, a 1984 Dodge Pierce*

*ASAP Vehicle*

*RFD ASAP 2*

*Bike Team*

*Quint 6, a 1998 Pierce*

53

# Engine House 7

*Steamer Company 7*

*Wagon Company 7*

Engine Company 7 embarked on its service on April 29, 1890, and was housed at 910 East Cary Street. The company was relocated in 1952 to 906 East Broad Street with Engine 3 beginning a series of transitions not seen by any other fire company in Richmond's history. Engine Company 7 was moved in April 1966 to 2505 Jefferson Davis Highway with Engine Company 21. It relocated again in July 1968 to 411 East Commerce Road with Engine Company 13. Engine Company 7 moved yet again on December 28, 1969 to 2915 Bainbridge Street with Engine Company 17. The company again relocated in April 1970 to 4715 Forest Hill Avenue with Engine Company 20. Engine Company 7's name was removed from the active fire companies list on July 1, 1972 when the company was redesignated as Flying Squad 2.

Engine House 7
910 East Cary Street

# ENGINE HOUSE 7

*1962 Mack*

## To keep ahead in fire protection Richmond adds still another Mack

**MACK**
FIRST NAME FOR
**FIRE APPARATUS**

*1959 Mack Ad RFD Engine 7*

*Engine 7, a 1955 Mack*

*Horse-Drawn Wagon 7*

*Engine Company 7*

55

# Engine House 8

In 1891, Engine Company 8 commenced service housed at 500 North Denny Street until 1951 when it was relocated to new quarters at 1018 Williamsburg Road where it remains today. On July 23, 1998, Engine 8 became Quint Company 8. Engine 8's apparatus was joined by a new Quint apparatus. Along with Station 21, Station 8 currently has an assigned foam unit tasked to respond in times of need throughout the City of Richmond. Now designated as Quint Company 8, its membership has served the city for 119 years.

*Engine House 8 at 1018 Williamsburg Road*

*Steamer 8, circa 1880's*

*Quint 8, a 1998 Rear Mount 75′ Aerial*

*Chief Joynes with a new 1939 GMC-Pirsch Hose Wagon 8*

*Foam Tanker 8*

*Heavy Rescue 2, a 1956 International*

*Engine House 8 at 500 North Denny Street*

56

# ENGINE HOUSE 8

*Engine Company 8*

*Engine Company 8 A-Shift*

*Quint Company 8 A-Shift*

*Engine Company 8 B-Shift*

*Quint Company 8 B-Shift*

*Engine Company 8 C-Shift*

*Quint Company 8 C-Shift*

# Engine House 9

*Engine House 9 at 801 North 5th Street*

*Wagon 9, an Ainslie Horse-Drawn Carriage*

*Steamer Company 9*

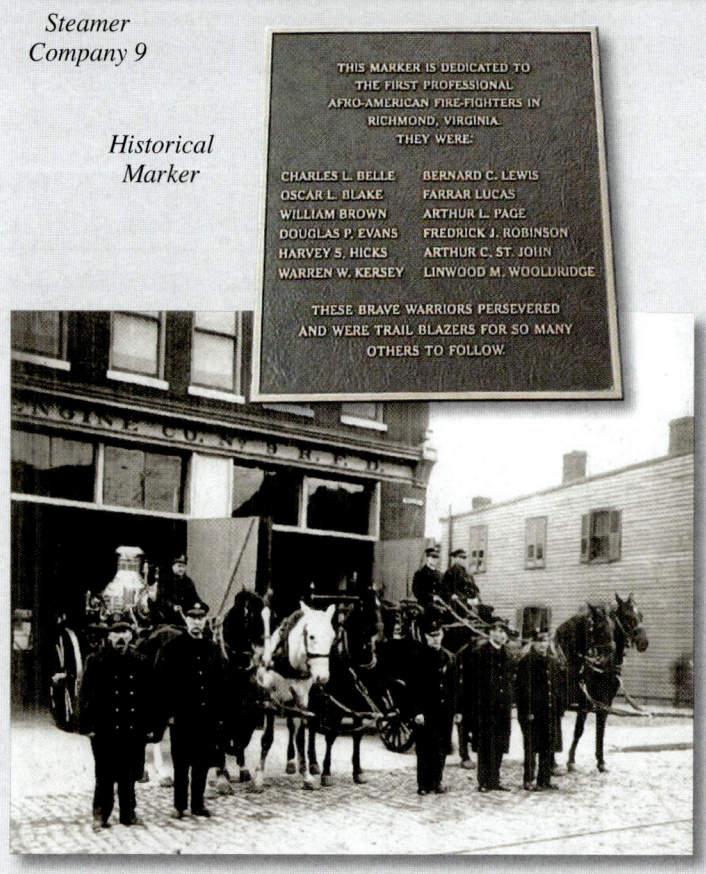

*Historical Marker*

Engine Company 9 was placed in service on October 16, 1902, housed at 801 North 5th Street. In 1950, the Richmond Fire Bureau hired its first 10 African American professional firefighters and assigned them to this company. They served together with pride, professionalism, honor, and integrity until 1963 when the department became integrated and many of Engine 9's members were reassigned. On March 20, 1968, Engine Company 9 moved to new quarters at 723 East Leigh Street with Engine Company 3. The company moved once again in July 1968 to new quarters at 411 North 6th Street with Engine 3. In 1970, the company moved one final time to 324 West Leigh Street with Engine 5. Engine Company 9 proudly served for 70 years until being disbanded on July 1, 1972.

*Engine Company 9 and Steamer 9*

# ENGINE HOUSE 9

*Wagon 9, a 1952 Oren*

## AFRICAN AMERICANS IN RICHMOND FIRE AND EMERGENCY SERVICES

In 1858, a paid fire department was organized in Richmond, Virginia. It consisted of six commanders, six foreman, and 90 firefighters. This Fire Brigade was placed under the supervision of a City Council Committee. On October 25, 1858, City Council authorized each company to use 10 slaves "of good character" to man the pumps. During this time a movement to replace hand-pumped engines with steamers gathered force. On January 5, 1864, the Council Fire Committee authorized the Fire Brigade to select one Negro man to act as hostler (a person who takes care of horses) and one Negro man to serve as a fireman (a person who fires and lubricates steam locomotives) for a steamer fire engine. It was May 5, 1950, when a local paper announced that the city personnel department would soon set in motion operations for the recruitment of Richmond's and the State of Virginia "first ten Negro firefighters." On July 1, 1950, the department hired its first "Negro" firefighters to form the first black unit in the city. The plan called for the men to work under white officers until they could qualify for promotion. Ten men were selected from 500 applicants. They were as follows: Charles L. Belle, William E. Brown, Douglas P. Evans, Harvey S. Hicks II, Warren W. Kersey, Bernard C. Lewis, Farrar Lucas, Arthur L. Page, Arthur C. St. John, and Linwood M. Wooldridge. Arthur C. St. John was called to return to the military in 1950 and Frederick J. Robinson was hired. When Farrar Lucas resigned in 1951 Oscar L. Blake was hired. The black firefighters would man Engine Company 9 at Fifth and Duval Streets "in the heart of a Negro residential and business district."

The qualifications for Negro firefighters were the same as for the white firefighters. However, white recruits would go immediately to the fire stations for company assignments and into regularly scheduled training classes, whereas a special training program was required for the Negro firefighters. The black firefighters were going into a single company house as a unit and under the leadership the "Drill Master" had to be completely trained in every detail before they could function as such. The black firefighters were trained for two months, twice the required time for white firefighters. Part of the reason the training was so long was the department erected separate sleeping quarters and bathrooms to house the four white officers and two white engineers. Black firefighters got most of the assignments to fight the constant dump fires and had to wash and clean the hoses for their own companies after a fire and sometimes for some of the white units at the scene. They were required to wash all the equipment after every run (while white companies washed equipment near the end of the shift). This meant that if they had six calls during a shift, they washed all the equipment six times. They were also required weekly to wash down the walls of the fire station from top to bottom, a task that white companies were not required to do. Black firefighters had to wear full dress uniforms (hat, coat, tie, dress shirt and pants) if they wanted to sit outside of the fire station. Therefore, if a fire call came and they were outside, they had to answer the call in dress uniforms. Other companies were not required to do this.

*Lt. Page and Captain Hicks*

**SA 54**
**ENGINE COMPANY NO. 9 FIRE STATION**

On 1 July 1950, the first professional Afro-American firefighters in Virginia were hired and in September were stationed on the northeast corner of this intersection. These courageous pioneers created a loyalty and dedication to each other and their profession notwithstanding discriminatory practices. Harvey S. Hicks, among those first hired, became the city's first black fire captain in September 1961. On 14 June 1963, Hicks and firefighter Douglas P. Evans sacrificed their lives in a rescue attempt. The city integrated the fire department on 6 July 1963 and demolished the fire station in 1968.

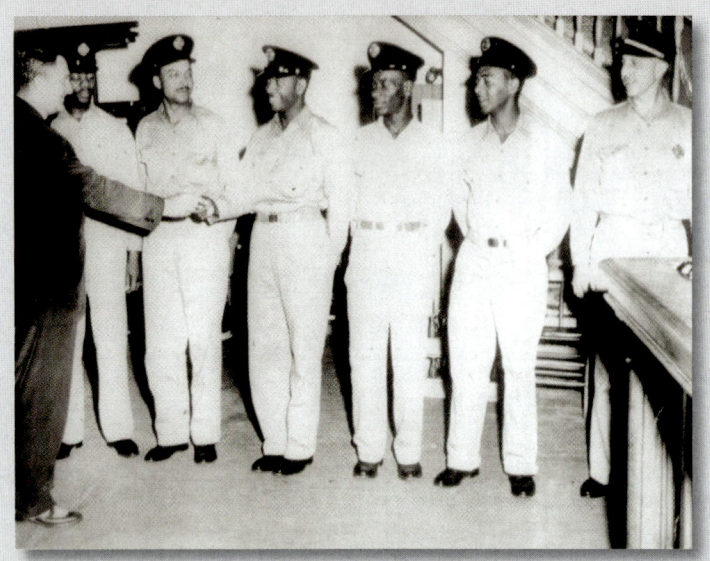

# ENGINE HOUSE 9

*First African American members of Engine Company 9*

*Engine 9 B-Shift*

*Engine 9 B-Shift in 1972*

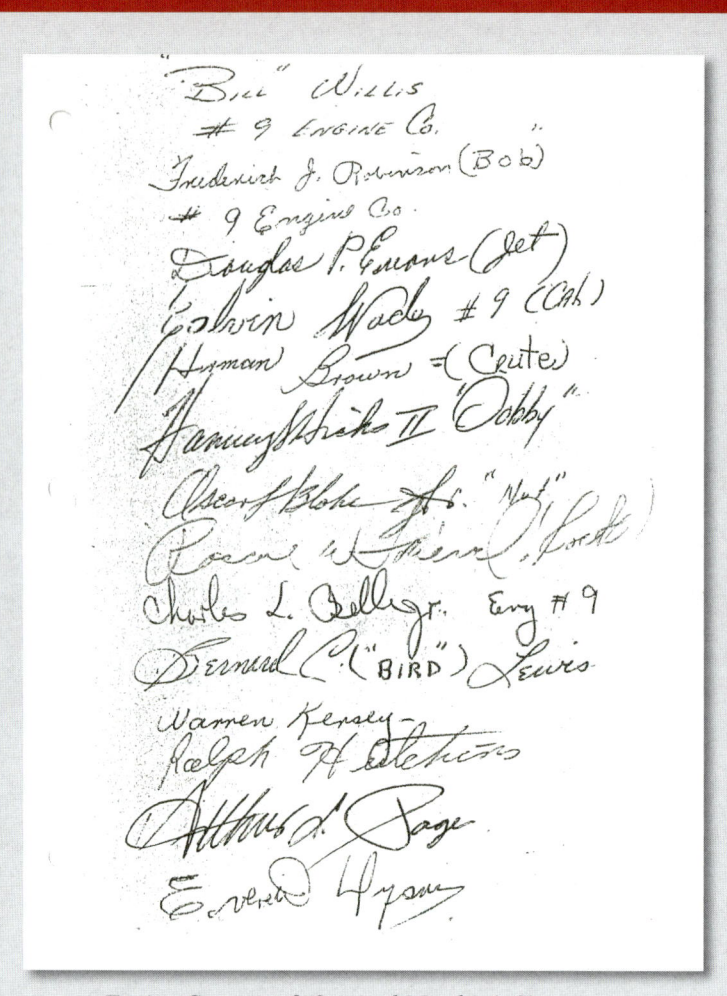

*Engine Company 9 Original Member's Signatures*

The men of Engine Company 9 were often given the chores nobody else wanted. Members were called to city property when grass needed to be cut, buildings needed to be painted, or hornets' nests needed to be removed. They also drove the service truck from station to station collecting damaged equipment and delivering laundry and supplies. They could not go into three of the city's fire stations, (6, 13, & 19). Instead they would go around to the back of the stations and knock on the window and white firemen would bring their laundry to the driver. One of the white captains said "They are good firefighters under proper leadership and they are doing well learning to drive the equipment". "On one or two occasions, he said that nervousness and over-eagerness hindered them". Despite feeling as though they were being treated like second-class citizens, they made up their minds that they would be the best firefighters the city had. They were the first group to be trained as a company; they could go into a fire and put it out scientifically. Although being college graduates or having some college, the black firefighters of Engine Company 9 were better educated and better trained than most of the city firefighters. But they were not afforded the same opportunities as their white counterparts.

Normally, it took three years to qualify for an engineering position (driver/pump). However, when some of the members of Engine Company 9 became qualified for the job, the position was mysteriously eliminated. Firefighters at Engine Company 9 always scored in the top 10 in examination scores, however, because of segregation they were not allowed to supervise white firefighters. Therefore, unless there was a vacancy in Engine Company 9 there were no promotion opportunities for black firefighters. Black firefighters were placed on promotion lists until the lists expired. Harvey S. Hicks was promoted to Lieutenant in 1955 and was assigned to E-9 and promoted to Captain in 1961 and assigned to E-9. Linwood M. Wooldridge was promoted to Lieutenant in 1956 and assigned to E-9. Oscar L. Blake was promoted to Lieutenant

# ENGINE HOUSE 9

in 1959 and also assigned to E-9. Arthur L. Page was promoted to Lieutenant in 1961 to replace Lt. Harvey S. Hicks and was also assigned to E-9. Charles L. Belle was promoted to Lieutenant in 1967 and was assigned to E-9. Charles L. Belle passed the Lieutenant's examination in 1956 but had to take the test 10 more times before he was promoted to the rank of Lieutenant in December, 1967.

The black firefighters remained segregated at Engine Company 9 until 1963. A tragedy struck in 1963 that caused the department to take another look at segregation. On June 14, 1963 Captain Harvey S. Hicks, Douglas P. Evans, and Calvin Wade attempted to rescue a self-employed contractor from a 23-feet deep pit. When the three failed to return, Herman Brown went down to see what had happened and saw that all four men had passed out. Feeling weak himself, Brown climbed back up the ladder. Lt. Oscar Blake went down next. Having just enough strength to pull off his mask, Lt. Blake climbed back up the ladder. By that time other firefighters had arrived, using air packs they brought Wade up, administered oxygen, and he regained consciousness. All Wade could remember was Captain Hicks was giving artificial respiration to the contractor. Captain Harvey S. Hicks, Firefighter Douglas P. Evans, and the contractor were pronounced deceased on arrival at St. Phillip's Hospital. Captain Harvey S. Hicks, the department's highest-ranking black officer and firefighter Douglas P. Evans suffocated in this rescue attempt of a contractor who was also a good friend of the firefighters. Since all the black firefighters were stationed together it was possible that a major catastrophe could possibly wipe out the company.

After 13 years, some type of action was taken to integrate six of the department's 28 companies with the departments' 13 black firefighters. Two black firefighters were assigned to each of the six fire companies and one assumed a fire communications position. On July 6, 1963, Bernard C. Lewis and Charles L. Belle Jr. were assigned to Engine Company 5. William W. Kersey and Herman O. Brown were assigned to Engine Company 17. Roscoe W. Friend and Frederick J. Robinson were assigned to Engine Company 12. Robert L. Myers and Calvin Wade were assigned to Engine Company 11. Ralph Hutchins was assigned to Truck Company 4. After a temporary assignment working out of the Chief's office, another first for blacks, Arthur C. St. John was assigned to the fire communications center in Monroe Park, which also was another first assignment for blacks. Lt. Oscar L. Blake and Lt. Arthur L. Page remained at Engine Company 9 under a white captain and over the white firefighters transferred to Engine Co 9. The black firefighters had consistently demonstrated competency and commitment to the department while battling subtle discrimination. Fire station No. 9 was built in 1902 and demolished in 1968. On Saturday, July 1, 2000, the Southwest Corner of 5th and Duval Street became a historical highway landmark.

*Engine 9 Responding*

# Engine House 10 & Truck 3

*Truck Company 3, a 1937 American LaFrance*

Engine Company 10 began service on July 1, 1905, the same day Truck Company 3 was reassigned to their station at 1609 West Broad Street. The engine and truck companies became Task Force 10 on June 28, 1993. When task forces were disbanded on May 25, 1996, the truck was taken out of service and the engine was reinstated as Engine Company 10. The company relocated to new quarters at 900 Hermitage Road on December 22, 1993 where it serves today. On February 12, 1998, Engine 10 was formed into Quint Company 10. Engine 10's apparatus was kept as Engine 10 and a new Quint apparatus was placed into service. Fire Station 10 currently houses Engine Company 10 and Rescue Company 2.

*Steamer House 10 at 1609 West Broad Sreet*

*Engine House 10*

*Current Station 10 at 900 Hermitage Road*

*Engine 10 A-Shift*

*Engine 10 B-Shift*

*Engine 10 C-Shift*

# Engine House 10 & Truck 3

*Quint 10 A-Shift*

*Quint 10 B-Shift*

*Quint 10 C-Shift*

Truck Company 3 began in 1889 at 200 S. Laurel Street as Hook and Ladder 3 with Steamer Company 6. On July 1, 1905, the truck company was reassigned to 1609 West Broad Street with a newly established Engine Company 10. Truck Company 3 and Engine 10 were combined to form Task Force 10 on June 28, 1993. When task forces were disbanded on May 25, 1996, the truck was taken out of service and the engine was reinstated as Engine Company 10.

*1965 Oren*

*1970 Maxim*

*1992 Seagrave*

*3 Truck, a 1960 Mack Pirsch*

*Truck 3, a 1971 American LaFrance.*

*Quint 10, a 1998 Pierce 105′ Aerial*

*Steamer 10 and Truck Company 3*

63

# Engine House 11 & Truck 4

On November 16, 1908, Engine Company 11 began service at 1235 North 28th Street. While a new station was constructed on the same site, Engine Company 11 relocated temporarily to 308 N. 24th Street with Engine 1. They returned to their new quarters until their in-house reassignment with Truck 4 as Task Force 11 (TF-11) on June 27, 1987. Task Force 11 continued to operate the engine and truck as a single unit until Task Forces were disbanded on May 25, 1996. Engine 11 remained in service at Station 11 while Truck 4 was placed out of service. On March 12, 1998, Engine 11 was formed into Quint Company 11. Engine 11's apparatus was sent to Engine 12, and a new Quint apparatus and First Response Vehicle (FRV) were placed into service at Station 11.

*Engine House 11 in 1977*

*Current Station 11*

*Engine 11, a 1968 Oren Pumper*

*Original Engine House 11 at 1235 N. 28th Street*

# ENGINE HOUSE 11 & TRUCK 4

*Engine 11 A-Shift*

*Quint 11 A-Shift*

*Engine 11 B-Shift*

*Quint 11 B-Shift*

*Engine 11 C-Shift*

*Quint 11 C-Shift*

Truck Company 4 began in 1909 and was housed with Engine Company 11 at 1235 North 28th Street. While a new station was built on the same site, the truck company operated out of Station 8 at 1018 Williamsburg Road from 1978 to 1979. Truck Company 4 returned to their new quarters until their in-house reassignment with Engine 11 as Task Force 11 (TF-11) on June 27, 1987. Task Force 11 continued to operate the engine and truck as a single unit until Task Forces were disbanded on May 25, 1996. Engine 11 remained in service at Station 11 while Truck 4 was placed out of service.

**FIRE STATION 11**
**1235 N. 28TH STREET**

*Quint 11 at North 26th Street Structure Fire*

65

# Engine House 12

**FIRE STATION 12**
**2223 W. CARY STREET**

*Engine House 12 at 2223 West Cary Street*

On November 16, 1908, Engine Company 12 began its long history at 2223 West Cary Street in Fire Station 12. As the Richmond Fire Department's oldest active fire station, Station 12 houses our department's last working fire pole. On December 1, 1998, Engine Company 12 was formed into Quint Company 12, adding a new Quint apparatus to the fire station.

*1950's Engine House 12*

*Modern Day Station 12*

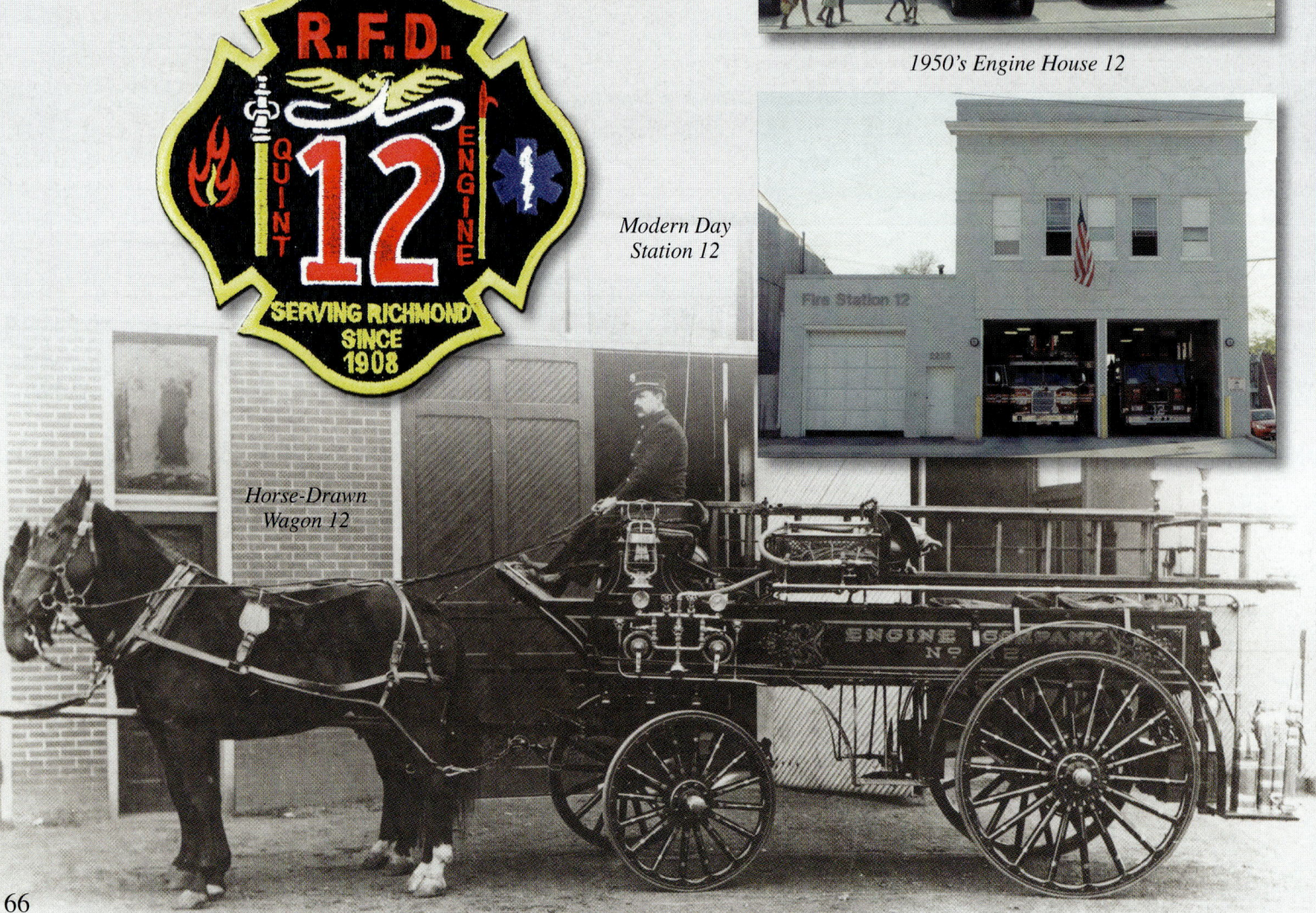

*Horse-Drawn Wagon 12*

66

# ENGINE HOUSE 12

*Engine Company 12*

*Engine company 12 B-Shift*

*Engine Company 12 C-Shift*

*Engine 12 Oren*

*Quint 12 A-Shift*

*1972 Maxim*

*Unit 99 Heavy Rescue, a 1977 International-Reading*

*Quint 12 B-Shift*

*Quint 12, a 1998 Pierce*

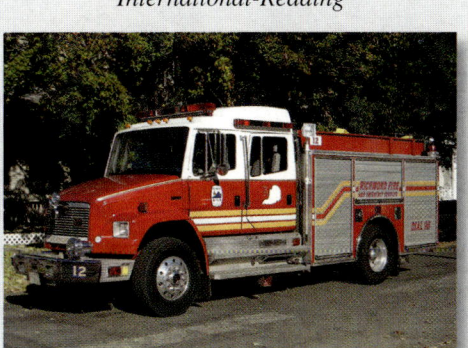

*FRV Engine 12*

*Quint 12 C-Shift*

67

# Rescue 1 & Dive Team

*Brush 1 with Zodiacs*

*Water Rescue 1, a 2006 International-Marion*

*Rescue 1*

On January 1, 1997, as a part of the Total Quint Concept, the Richmond Fire Department placed into service three heavy rescue companies. At least one rescue company responds to all major incidents in order to provide specialized equipment and expertise, conduct search and rescue, and perform in-depth extrication should it be needed. In addition to their normal duties, Rescue 1 functions as the City of Richmond's only water rescue team, known informally as "The Dive Team." Rescue 1 maintains an on-duty team of personnel trained as divers and swift water rescue technicians to respond to emergency water related rescues, recovery incidents, evidence collection, mutual aid, or any other type of water incident wherein the team is deemed necessary. To successfully accomplish their assigned duties, the team utilizes a number of different types and sizes of inflatable boats; specialized water-to-land communication equipment; several boat trailers; a 2005 International/Marion walk-through rescue vehicle known as Dive 1; and a reconfigured brush truck known as Dive 2. The Water Rescue Team is currently housed with Quint 1 and Battalion 1 at 308 N. 24th Street.

*Rescue 1 RFD Ambulance*

*Rescue Boat*

# Rescue 1 & Dive Team

*Water Rescue Training*

*Dive Team*

*Rescue 1 and Quint 1 A-Shift*

*Rescue 1 B-Shift*

*Search and Recovery*

*Rescue 1 C-Shift*

*Rescue 1 B-Shift*

*Rescue 1 C-Shift*

*Water Rescue on the James River*

*Drag Bar*

71

# Rescue 2 & Technical Rescue Team

*1982 Mack CF Pumper*

*Rescue 2, a 1998 Pierce*

*High Angle Rescue Downtown*

Rescue Company 2 is the Richmond Fire Department's Technical Rescue Team (TRT). They provided specialized rescue services of a technical nature to the citizens of Richmond. These services include but are not limited to: High and low angle vertical rescue, confined space rescue, elevator incidents, and structural collapse. To complete their assigned duties Rescue 2 uses a specially equipped medium duty box truck in addition to their Pierce Quantum Rescue Truck. Rescue Company 2 was created as a new fire company under the Richmond Fire Department's Total Quint Concept, and went into service on January 1, 1997. The Technical Rescue Team is currently housed with Quint 10 at 914 Hermitage Road.

# Rescue 2 & Technical Rescue Team

*Rescue 2 A-Shift*

*Rescue 2 B-Shift*

*Rescue 2 C-Shift*

*Rescue 2 A-Shift*

*Rescue 2 B-Shift*

*Rescue 2 C-Shift*

*Rope Training*

*High Angle Training at the Richmond Coliseum*

*Hunt Avenue, January 20, 2009*

73

# Rescue 3 & Hazardous Materials Team

*Decon*

*Haz-Mat Unit, a 1989 Peterbilt*

On January 1, 1997, the third of the three heavy rescue companies, Rescue 3, was placed into service as part of the Total Quint Concept. In addition to their normal duties Rescue 3 operated as the Richmond Fire Department's Hazardous Material Team. Originally formed in 1983, the team was comprised of personnel from Engine Company 13 and Ladder Company 5, who cross-trained together from their shared assignment at Station 13 at 411 East Commerce Road. The team is now comprised of the members of Rescue 3 and Quint 13 and continues to operate from Fire Station 13. In addition to their Pierce Quantum Rescue truck, the hazmat team also utilizes a medium duty box truck known as Hazmat 2, and a 1989 Peterbilt/Marion Hazardous Material Unit known as Hazmat 3.

*Rescue 3*

# Rescue 3 & Hazardous Materials Team

*Rescue 3 A-Shift*

*Rescue 3 B-Shift*

*Rescue 3 C-Shift*

*Rescue 3 A-Shift*

*Quint 13 and Rescue 3 B-Shift*

*Rescue 3 C-Shift*

*Early Haz-Mat Mitigation*

*White Powder Incident*

*Pool Training*

# Engine House 13 & Truck 5

In 1910, Engine Company 13 was placed in service at 10th and Hull Streets until moving to new quarters at 1000 and 1002 Bainbridge Street on July 21, 1911. Engine Company House 13 was the only firehouse in Richmond's history to carry separate addresses in the same building. The engine company was joined by Truck Company 5 in 1913. They both moved into the current Station 13 at 411 East Commerce Road in July of 1968. On January 1, 1997, in an in-house transfer Engine Company 13's personnel were reassigned to the newly formed Rescue Company 3. Rescue 3 used a reserve apparatus and brush truck until their newly ordered Pierce Rescue Truck was placed into service in November of 1997. Truck Company 5 continued to operate as a truck company until February of 1998 when Quint 13, a new 105′ aerial ladder, was received by the fire department. Truck Company 5 was then disbanded and many of its members, along with other department personnel, were reassigned to the new Quint Company 13. Engine 13's apparatus was sent to Engine 25, and Truck 5's apparatus was sent to the auto shop for disposal. In 2007, Quint 13's aerial was sent to Quint Company 1 and replaced with Quint 5's 100′ aerial platform. Fire Station 13 currently houses Quint Company 13 and Rescue Company 3.

*Engine 13 and Truck 5 on Bainbridge Street*

*New quarters in 1968 at 411 E. Commerce Road*

*Current Station 13*

*Steamer 13 and Truck 5 when first formed in 1911*

# Engine House 13 & Truck 5

*Rescue Boat 1 at Bainbridge Station*

*Quint 13 Rear Mount Aerial Platform*

Truck Company 5 began in 1913, joining Engine Company 13 at 1000 and 1002 Bainbridge Street. This was the only fire house in Richmond's history to carry two separate addresses in the same building. Relocating along with Engine Company 13, they moved to new quarters at 411 E. Commerce Road. After serving with Engine 13 for 30 years from this location, Truck Company 5 was disbanded in February 1998 when the majority of its personnel were reassigned to Quint Company 13.

*13 A-Shift*

*13 B-Shift*

*13 C-Shift*

*Quint 13 A-Shift*

*Quint 13 B-Shift*

*Quint 13 C-Shift*

# Station 14 & Truck 6

*Station 14 in 1922*

*Engine 14, a 1948 Mack*

*1976 Mack*

*1989 KME*

*1991 Ford-Pierce*

*1998 FRV*

*Midi-Pumper 14*

**E**ngine Company 14 went into service during 1914 at Roberts Street between North and Barton Avenues. On May 1, 1923, it was assigned to new quarters at 2932 Hawthorne Avenue. The engine company temporarily worked out of Station 16 at 3901 Chamberlayne Avenue from February 1, 1982 to July 24, 1983 while Station 14 was being rebuilt at the same location. On September 17, 1996, Engine 14 and Truck 6 combined to form Quint Company 14 when Richmond purchased its first Quint apparatus.

*Current Station 14 at 2934 Hawthorne Avenue*

# Station 14 & Truck 6

*1964 Mack*

*1977 Seagrave*

*Quint 14, a 1996 Ferrara HME 75' Aerial*

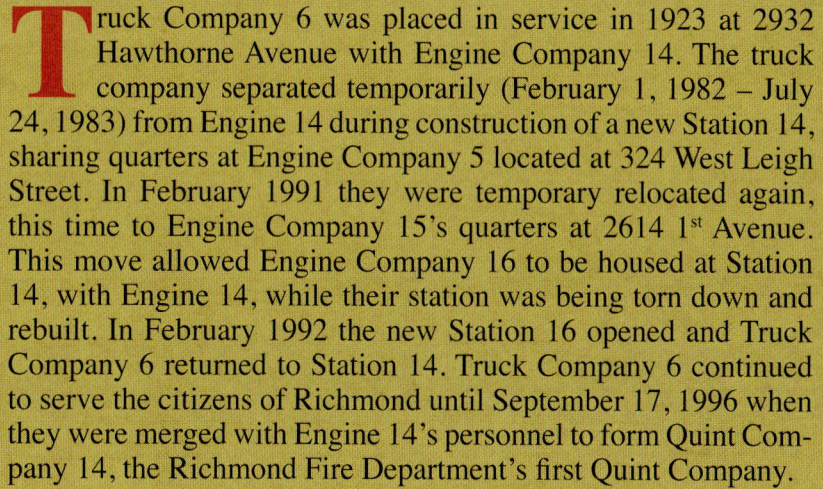

**T**ruck Company 6 was placed in service in 1923 at 2932 Hawthorne Avenue with Engine Company 14. The truck company separated temporarily (February 1, 1982 – July 24, 1983) from Engine 14 during construction of a new Station 14, sharing quarters at Engine Company 5 located at 324 West Leigh Street. In February 1991 they were temporary relocated again, this time to Engine Company 15's quarters at 2614 1st Avenue. This move allowed Engine Company 16 to be housed at Station 14, with Engine 14, while their station was being torn down and rebuilt. In February 1992 the new Station 16 opened and Truck Company 6 returned to Station 14. Truck Company 6 continued to serve the citizens of Richmond until September 17, 1996 when they were merged with Engine 14's personnel to form Quint Company 14, the Richmond Fire Department's first Quint Company.

*Quint 14 A-Shift*

*Quint 14 B-Shift*

*Quint 14 C-Shift*

*Quint 14 A-Shift*

*Quint 14 B-Shift*

*Quint 14 C-Shift*

# Station 15

Current Station 15 at 2614 1st Avenue

Station 15 in 1943

In 1914 Engine Company 15 was formed and placed into service at 3011 Meadowbridge Road. Fire Station 15 was torn down and rebuilt at the same location in 1923. On April 27, 1990, Engine Company 15 was relocated to a new Fire Station 15 at 2614 1st Avenue from where they serve today. Engine Company 15 became Quint Company 15 on May 1, 1998, replacing their apparatus with a new Quint apparatus and First Response Vehicle (FRV). Their old apparatus was sent to the auto shop for disposal.

Engine 15, a 1952 Mack

Old Station 15 at 3011 Meadowbridge Road

# STATION 15

Engine 15 A-Shift

Engine 15 B-Shift

Engine 15 C-Shift

Quint 15 A-Shift

Quint 15 B-Shift

Quint 15 C-Shift

Engine 15 FRV

1987 Maxim

Quint 15 Working

81

# Station 16

Engine Company 16 went into service in 1914, and continues to service the City of Richmond from their original location at 3901 Chamberlayne Avenue. They have been relocated several times over the years for construction. Their 1st relocation was to Engine Company 15's quarters at 3011 Meadowbridge Road to allow Engine 14 to temporary use their station while Station 14 was being rebuilt. Engine 16 returned to their quarters on July 24, 1983. In February 1991, Engine 16 was relocated to Engine 14's quarters at 2932 Hawthorne Avenue, so Station 16 could be torn down and rebuilt. The company moved into the new Station 16 in February 1992, where it remains today. On July 27, 1998, Engine 16 was formed into Quint Company 16. Engine Company 16's apparatus was kept as Engine 16, and a new Quint apparatus was placed into service.

*Station 16 in 1914*

*Station 16 in 1943*

*Station 16 in 1970's*

*Current Station 16 at 3901 Chamberlayne Avenue*

## STATION 16

Engine 16 A-Shift

Engine 16 B-Shift

Engine 16 C-Shift

Quint 16 A-Shift

Quint 16 B-Shift

Puff

Engine 16, a 1952 Mack

1989 KME

Quint 16, a 1998 Pierce

Pumper 16, a 1921 Brockway-American LaFrance

83

# Station 17

## FIRE STATION 17
### 2901 BAINBRIDGE STREET

*Current Station 17*

Beginning its service in 1915 at 2901 Bainbridge Street, Engine Company 17 still remains housed there today. On August 7, 1998, Engine 17 became Quint Company 17, adding a new Quint apparatus to their existing engine. Station 17 is the oldest active firehouse on Southside and the 2nd oldest in the Richmond Fire Department. In 2010 the City of Richmond received a 3.2 million dollar federal stimulus grant to assist with the construction of a new Fire Station 17.

*Engine Company 17 in 1956*

*Station 17 in 1943*

# STATION 17

*Engine 17 A-Shift*

*Engine 17 B-Shift*

*Engine 17 C-Shift*

*Quint 17 A-Shift*

*Quint 17 B-Shift*

*Quint 17 C-Shift*

*Wagon 17, a 1948 Mack and Engine 17, a 1953 Mack*

*Quint 17, a 1998 Pierce*

# Station 18 & Truck 7

*Station 18 in 1943*

*Station 18*

Engine Company 18 initiated service in 1939 at 412 North Thompson Street where it continues to serves from today. On August 13, 1998, Engine 18 placed into service a First Response Vehicle (FRV) 18. Old Engine 18 was sent to Engine Company 8 to use as their engine. On December 1, 1998, Engine 18 was formed into Quint Company 18. A new Quint apparatus was added and placed into service with the FRV serving as Engine 18. Quint 18 was the last Quint placed into service by the Richmond Fire Department, and officially completed the Department's transition to the Total Quint Plan. Station 18 is also the chief's quarters for the Battalion 2.

*Station 18 at 412 N. Thompson Street*

86

# Station 18 & Truck 7

*Engine 18, a 1970 Maxim*

*1987 Maxim*

*Truck 7, an Oren-Pirsch*

*1988 Seagrave 100' Aerial*

Established in 1939, Truck Company 7 is set apart in history by being assigned to Station 18, at 412 North Thompson Street, for its entire length of service. Perhaps an even greater distinction is Truck Company 7 was the last ladder company in the Richmond Fire Department. On August 20, 1998, Truck Company 7 merged with Engine 18 to form Quint Company 18.

*Quint 18, a 75' Aerial*

*FRV 18*

*Midi Pumper 18, a 2006 Pierce Contender*

*Engine 18 A-Shift*

*Engine 18 B-Shift*

*Engine 18 C-Shift*

*Quint 18 A-Shift*

*Quint 18 B-Shift*

*Quint 18 C-Shift*

# Station 19

Current Station 19 at 311 Maple Avenue

Engine 19 crew in 1940

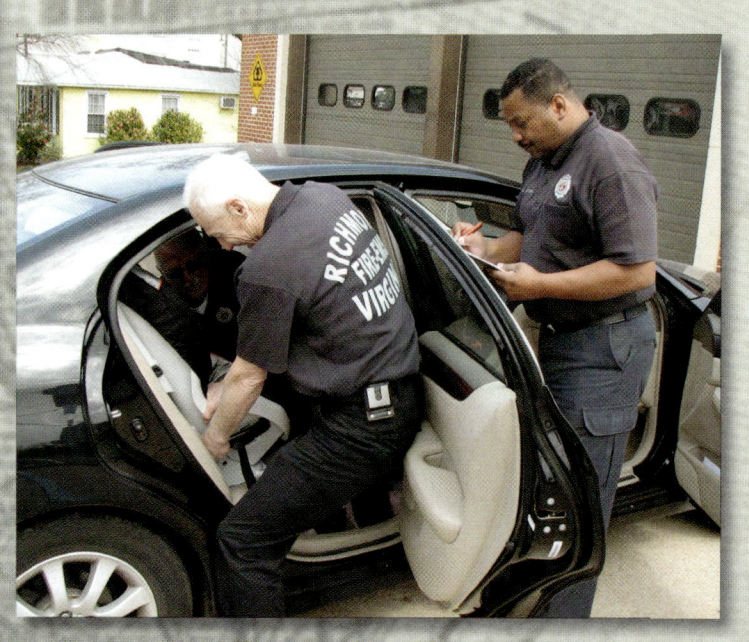

Child Safety Seat Install

Engine House 19 in 1943

# STATION 19

In 1941, the City of Richmond annexed the Westhampton area of Henrico County. This area included the Westhampton Volunteer Fire Department Station located at 313 Maple Avenue. This station became Richmond Fire Station 19, and the volunteer chief became Station 19's first captain. In 1952, Engine 19 moved one door down to its new quarters at 311 Maple Avenue where it remains today. On June 28, 1998, Engine 19 was formed into Quint Company 19. Engine 19's apparatus was kept as Engine 19 and a new Quint apparatus was placed into service.

*Oren Wagon 19*

*1972 Maxim*

*1977 American LaFrance*

*1990 KME*

*Brush 19, a 1991 Ford Pierce*

*Attack 19, a 1984 GMC Grumman*

*Quint 19, a 1998 Pierce*

*Engine 19 A-Shift*

*Engine 19 B-Shift*

*Engine 19 C-Shift*

*Quint 19 A-Shift*

*Quint 19 B-Shift*

*Quint 19 C-Shift*

# Station 20

*Brand New Station 20*

In 1943, Engine Company 20 began service at Station 20 at 4715 Forest Hill Avenue where it remains in service today. Doubling as a partial museum, Station 20 has housed and displayed retired Water Tower 1, a 1922 Seagrave 65 foot steel tower apparatus since August 19, 1998. Water Tower 1 is one of only thirteen built by Seagrave. On October 20, 1998, Engine 20 became Quint Company 20. Engine 20's apparatus was replaced with a new FRV and Quint apparatus.

*Engine 20, a 1942 Mack 80LS Pumper*

*Current Station 20 at 4715 Forest Hill Avenue*

# STATION 20

*1974 Mack*

*1988 KME*

*Retired 1922 Seagrave Water Tower 1, Currently Housed at Station 20*

*Quint 20, a 1998 Pierce*

*FRV 20*

*Engine 20 A-Shift*

*Engine 20 B-Shift*

*Engine 20 C-Shift*

*Quint 20 A-Shift*

*Quint 20 B-Shift*

*Quint 20 C-Shift*

91

# Station 21

Engine 21, a 1964 Mack

Foam 21, a 1969 Oren Foam Pumper

1977 American LaFrance

Foam 21, a 1988 GMC National

Station 21 at 2505 Jefferson Davis Highway

Engine Company 21 began in 1943 at 2505 Jefferson Davis Highway where it remains in service today. On July 29, 1998, Engine Company 21 became Quint Company 21. Engine 21's Seagrave apparatus was sent to Station 24 and re-designated as Engine 24. Subsequently, a new Quint and FRV apparatus were put into service. Due to its close proximity to the annexed portion of the city, Station 21 was one of the first stations to house a designated foam unit to respond in times of need throughout the City of Richmond.

1993 Seagrave

FRV 21

Quint 21, a 1998 Pierce 75' Aerial

92

# STATION 21

*Engine 21 A-Shift*

*Engine 21 B-Shift*

*Engine 21 C-Shift*

*Quint 21 A-Shift*

*Quint 21 B-Shift*

*Quint 21 C-Shift*

*Capt. D. Jewell*

*Quint 21*

# Station 22 & Truck 8

*Station 22 at 2420 Broad Rock Boulevard*

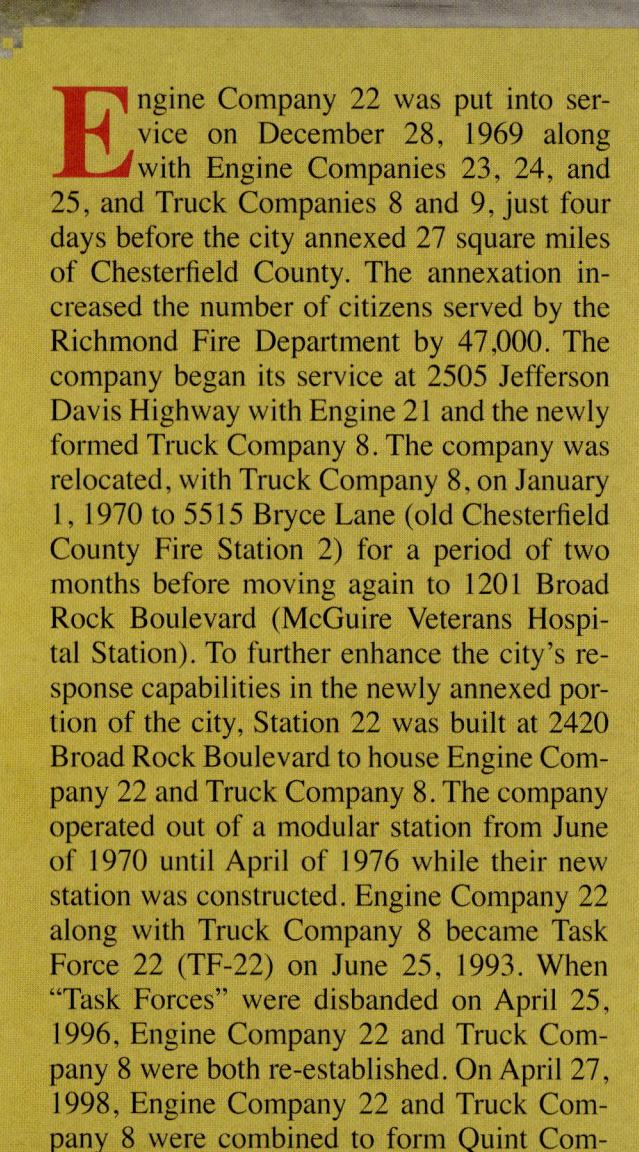

Engine Company 22 was put into service on December 28, 1969 along with Engine Companies 23, 24, and 25, and Truck Companies 8 and 9, just four days before the city annexed 27 square miles of Chesterfield County. The annexation increased the number of citizens served by the Richmond Fire Department by 47,000. The company began its service at 2505 Jefferson Davis Highway with Engine 21 and the newly formed Truck Company 8. The company was relocated, with Truck Company 8, on January 1, 1970 to 5515 Bryce Lane (old Chesterfield County Fire Station 2) for a period of two months before moving again to 1201 Broad Rock Boulevard (McGuire Veterans Hospital Station). To further enhance the city's response capabilities in the newly annexed portion of the city, Station 22 was built at 2420 Broad Rock Boulevard to house Engine Company 22 and Truck Company 8. The company operated out of a modular station from June of 1970 until April of 1976 while their new station was constructed. Engine Company 22 along with Truck Company 8 became Task Force 22 (TF-22) on June 25, 1993. When "Task Forces" were disbanded on April 25, 1996, Engine Company 22 and Truck Company 8 were both re-established. On April 27, 1998, Engine Company 22 and Truck Company 8 were combined to form Quint Company 22. Engine 22's apparatus was sent to Engine 8, and Truck 8's apparatus was sent to the auto shop for disposal. A new Quint apparatus and First Response Vehicle (FRV) were placed into service.

*Engine 22, a 1970 Maxim*

*1982 Mack*

*Truck 8, a 1982 Continental 100′ rear mount aerial*

94

## STATION 22 & TRUCK 8

Housed with Engine Company 21 at 2505 Jefferson Davis Highway for four days, Truck Company 8 began its service to the City of Richmond on December 28, 1969. On January 1, 1970, Truck Company 8 and Engine 22 were relocated to 5515 Bryce Lane. Truck Company 8 accompanied Engine Company 22 through various relocations until finally settling in at the newly built station at 2420 Broad Rock Boulevard in 1976. The company ran out of that house until Truck Company 8 was disbanded and turned into Task Force 22 (TF-22) on June 25, 1993. When "Task Forces" were disbanded on April 25, 1996, Truck Company 8 was re-established. They continued to run as a truck company until merging with Engine Company 22 on April 27, 1998, when Quint Company 22 was formed.

*Truck 8, an American LaFrance Tiller Truck*

*Seagrave Truck 8*

*1989, a KME*

*Quint 22, a 1998 Pierce 75′ Aerial*

*FRV 22, a 1998 Freightliner*

*Brush 22*

*Station 22 A-Shift*

*Station 22 B-Shift*

*Station 22 C-Shift*

*Quint 22 A-Shift*

*Quint 22 B-Shift*

*Quint 22 C-Shift*

# Station 23

Like the other annexation companies, Engine Company 23 was placed in service December 28, 1969. The company shared quarters with Engine Company 17 at 2915 Bainbridge Street for four days until relocating to 1239 Blakemore Road (old Chesterfield County Forrest View Station 9). The company found themselves in new temporary quarters again in July 1970 at 400 La Brook Concourse while a new fire station was constructed. The company took possession of the new station in May 1973 at 495 La Brook Concourse where it remains active today. On October 14, 1998, Engine Company 23 became Quint Company 23. A new Quint apparatus and First Response Vehicle (FRV) were added to Station 23, and the old apparatus was placed on reserve status as Engine 27 at Fire Training until its later disposal. Station 23 also serves as the chief quarters for Battalion 3.

*Old Engine House 23 at 1239 Blakemore Road Former Chesterfield Station 9*

*Station 23*

*Fire Communications Unit-90, a 1969 Chevrolet*

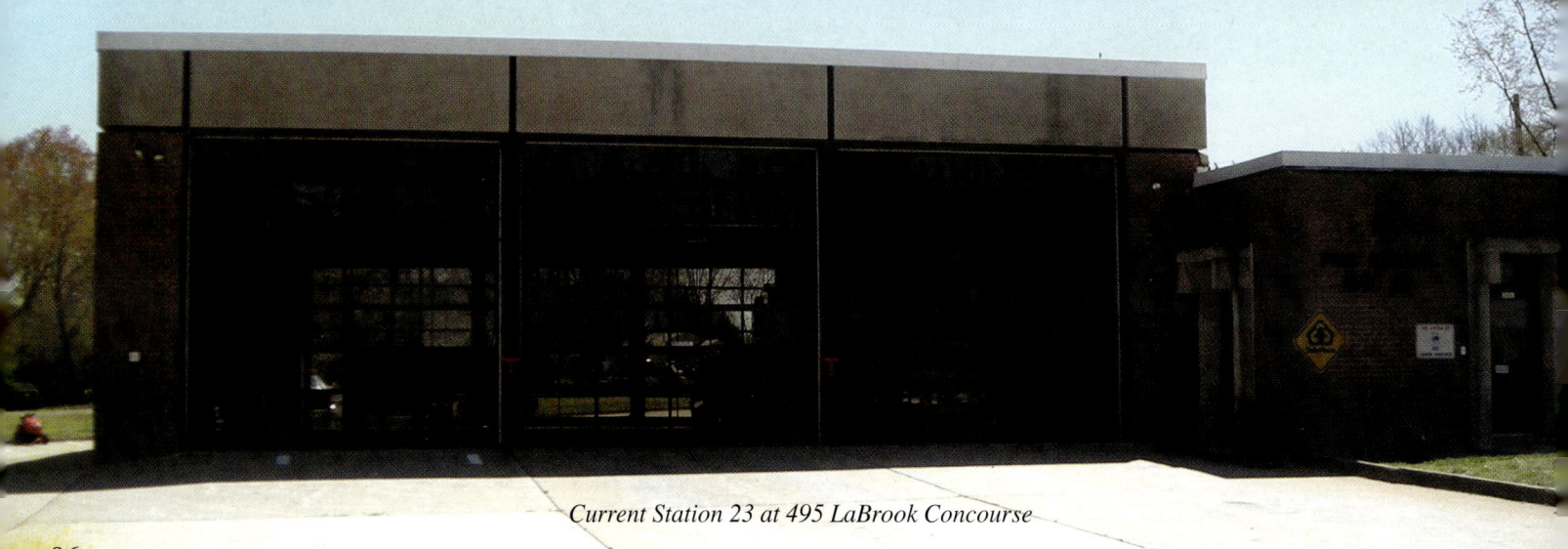

*Current Station 23 at 495 LaBrook Concourse*

# STATION 23

Brush 23, a 1970 International

1988 KME Firefox

Engine Company 23 A-Shift

Tanker 23, a 1970 Oren

Engine 23, a 1970 Maxim

Engine Company 23 C-Shift

Quint 23

Quint 23 A-Shift

Quint 23 B-Shift

FRV 23, a 1998 Freightliner

Quint 23 C-Shift

# Station 24 & Truck 9

*Temporary Station 24 at 7410 Forest Hill Avenue*

*Truck 9 and Engine 24 in Front of Brand New Station 24*

Awaiting annexation, Engine Company 24 went into service on December 28, 1969, at 4715 Forest Hill Avenue with Engine Company 20. The company moved to temporary quarters in July 1970 at 7410 Forest Hill Avenue until they moved just five doors down to their new and current quarters at 7400 Forest Hill Avenue in June of 1975. On April 2, 1998, Engine 24 and Truck 9 were combined to form Quint Company 24. Engine Company 24 received Engine Company 21's engine and a new Quint apparatus. Engine 24 sent their engine to the Fire Academy to serve as Engine 26, which allowed the academy to dispose of their older engine. Truck 9 was sent to the auto shop for disposal. In 2007, a new foam tanker apparatus was also placed in service at Station 24 to further enhance the city's capabilities of fire suppression.

*Current Station 24 at 7400 Forest Hill Avenue*

*Engine 24 A-Shift*

*Truck 9 B-Shift*

*Engine 24 C-Shift*

# Station 24 & Truck 9

*Quint 24 A-Shift*

*Quint 24 B-Shift*

*Quint 24 C-Shift*

In preparation of the annexation, the city put Truck Company 9 into service on December 28, 1969 at Station 20 at 4715 Forest Hill Avenue along with Engine Companies 20 and 24. Truck Company 9 and Engine Company 24 moved together to temporary quarters and remained there for almost five years until moving into the newly built Station 24 at 7400 Forest Hill Avenue. Both companies served together until April 2, 1998, when Truck Company 9 and Engine Company 24 were merged to form Quint Company 24.

*Tanker 24*

*Engine 24, a 1970 Maxim*

*Foam Tanker 24*

*Truck 9, a 1988 Seagrave 100' aerial*

*Truck 9 Mack Tiller*

*Engine 24, a 1993 Seagrave*

*Quint 24*

*American LaFrance, Truck 9*

99

# Station 25

*Newly Built Station 25*

*Engine 25, a 1970 Maxim pumper*

*Current Station 25 at 8800 W. Huguenot Road*

100

# STATION 25

Engine Company 25 was put into service on December 28, 1969, working out of 311 Maple Avenue with Engine Company 19. Awaiting completion of their new station in May 1972, the company worked from temporary modular quarters at 8800 West Huguenot Road within the newly annexed area. On July 3, 1998, Engine Company 25 became Quint Company 25. Engine 25's apparatus remained and was joined by a new Quint. In 2007, Quint 25 and Quint 21 were permanently swapped to reduce mileage concerns. Both Quints had their markings updated to reflect their new assignments.

*Brush 25, a 1970 International*

*1982 Mack Pumper*

*Engine 25, a 1990 KME*

*Quint 25, a 1998 Pierce Aerial*

*Engine 25 A-Shift*

*Engine 25 B-Shift*

*Engine 25 C-Shift*

*Quint 25 A-Shift*

*Quint 25 B-Shift*

*Quint 25 C-Shift*

# Closed Fire Houses & Disbanded Companies

*The following companies were disbanded for various reasons and now no longer serve the City of Richmond. Let us not forget their service and sacrifice to the city and its' citizens.*

| | |
|---|---|
| Engine Company 4 | June 26, 1971 |
| Engine Company 9 | July 1, 1972 |
| Engine Company 7 | July 1, 1972 |
| Engine Company 2 | January 1, 1973 |
| Engine Company 3 | July 1, 1981 |
| Tactical Squad 1 | July 1, 1981 |
| Truck Company 4 | June 27, 1987 |
| Truck Company 3 | June 28, 1993 |
| Truck Company 8 | June 28, 1993 |
| Tactical Squad 2 | June 10, 1995 |
| Task Force 10 | May 25, 1996 |
| Task Force 11 | May 25, 1996 |
| Task Force 22 | May 25, 1996 |
| Truck Company 6 | September 17, 1996 |
| Truck Company 1 | January 6, 1998 |
| Truck Company 5 | January 29, 1998 |
| Truck Company 2 | February 19, 1998 |
| Truck Company 8 | April 27, 1998 |
| Truck Company 7 | August 20, 1998 |

# Badges of the Richmond Fire Department

*Hook and Ladder Company 2*

# Administration

*Fire Headquarters at 908 E. Broad Street*

*Current Fire Headquarters, at 201 E. Franklin Street*

As the fire service has grown, so has the need to maintain the day to day requirements of that force. The members of fire administration handle the inner workings of the department and serve as the hub for the many situations that arise. From procurement to safety, and prevention to investigations, the day to day business of maintaining the Richmond Fire Department and its' 400 plus members operating at peak efficiency can be a daunting task. Located at 201 East Franklin Street, Fire Headquarters houses the Chief of Fire and his administrative staff. As fire department business is conducted and decisions are made, that information is disseminated through the respective battalion chiefs ultimately to the station captains and company officers in the field.

*First Motorized Chief's Car, a 1911 Knox*

# ADMINISTRATION

Chief Finnegan Jr. Awards Best Company Award

Battalion Chief Promotions

Joy C. Haynesworth and Kimberly Wilson-Cho

PIO Lt. Shawn Jones

# Fire Prevention Division

Established in 1920 by then Assistant Chief, L. S. Jones, the Fire Prevention Division is dedicated to the protection of life and property. Personnel are assigned to one of four sections; Community Programs, Fire Safety Inspections, Fire Investigations, and Hazardous Materials. They are guided by three principles – *Education – Engineering – Enforcement*. *Education* is the primary focus of day to day activities. A better informed individual will understand the important of creating a safer environment and overall make good decisions in an emergency. Through this pro-active effort, we hope to lessen the number of incidents or at the very least, the severity. It certainly transcends all four sections of the Division. *Engineering* is important to understand the appropriate design, application, and construction of building components. It is utilized through the development and application of local, state, and national codes, standards, and ordinances. Sound industry principles, past experiences, and laboratory tests are the basis for these documents. Understanding the science of fire is a key factor for staff to effectively carryout their responsibilities. *Enforcement*, though a last resort, is an avenue to ensure the building environment and associated activities meet an acceptable safe standard. It is hoped that through education, we will be able to obtain voluntary compliance.

Collectively, employing these principles and working closely with our customers will allow us to move one step closer to our goal of improving fire and life safety for our community.

*Free Smoke Detector program saves lives*

*Fire Inspections and Code Enforcement*

# FIRE PREVENTION DIVISION

*Tuck the Clown*

*Fire Safety House Demonstration*

*Lt. William Andrews*

*"Pluggie", Chief Currie, and Capt. Vida*

*Lt. Anthony Jones*

# Fire Prevention Division

*Fire Extinguisher Training Simulator*

*Fire Prevention Division with Chief Horton*

*Fire Marshal Response Vehicle*

*Sparky Entertains the Kids*

108

# Fire Prevention Division

*Capt. Tina Watkins*

*Puppet Show and Fire Safety Lesson*

*Christmas Family, 2009*

*Fire Prevention Team Members*

*Fire and Life Safety Trailer*

# INVESTIGATIONS UNIT

*Richmond Fire Investigations Unit*

*Determining Cause and Origin*

The Virginia Department of Fire Programs in coordination with the Virginia Fire Marshalls Office devised a program to train experienced fire department members who possess the aptitude and demeanor for police work with the skills to investigate cause and origin, recognize the signs of arson, collect and document evidence, investigate to identify the criminal, make the arrest, and process and present the case in court. Ideally this unit is made up of both police and fire department members. In this manner when the investigator/detective needs assistance from either side, the corresponding member from the department can "open the door" and access their own department's services for their counterpart. Richmond went to this system over 30 years ago with great success. While the faces have changed over the years, the mission remains clear: To determine fire cause and origin as well as bring to justice those who have broken the law.

# INVESTIGATIONS UNIT

Capt. M. Martin

Detective H. Gittman

Lt. A. Roberts

Lt. S. Brown

Investigator L. Archer

Investigator T. Chenault

**RICHMOND FIRE INVESTIGATIONS UNIT**

*The Investigations Division with Fire Chief Creecy and Fire Marshal Creasy*

# INVESTIGATIONS UNIT

*Bailey*

*Capt. Martin and Bailey*

## BAILEY

Joining the Richmond Fire Department in September, 1998, Bailey has become both a fixture and somewhat of a mascot to our department. A purebred Black Labrador Retriever, she is known by most school age children from her appearances in schools and at the Children's Hospital Safety Day, which she and her handler, Captain Mike Martin, have attended every year since her arrival. They have traveled as far east as Richmond County, as far south as Prince George County, as far west as Wintergreen, and as far north as Caroline County. She has assisted Henrico, Hanover, and Chesterfield on a regular basis as she was the first accelerant detection K9 in this area for many years.

Bailey retired in May of 2010, having assisted numerous fire investigations and investigators throughout the state. She has generated enormous amounts of good will and publicity for our department. There have been countless news stories on her and this department because of the uniqueness of what she does. She was awarded the commendation medal by Fire Chief Robert Creecy at the 2009 Richmond Fire Department Awards Ceremony. Bailey and her partner/handler, Captain Martin, have built a bond that will carry on far into her retirement. Her great service and enthusiasm will surely be missed by all in our ranks.

*Capt. Martin and Bailey work a fire scene.*

# INVESTIGATIONS UNIT

*Lt. Roberts investigates a fire scene in North Richmond.*

*Lt. Brown briefs law enforcement on a suspected arsonist.*

*Lt. O. Morris*

# Fire Training Division

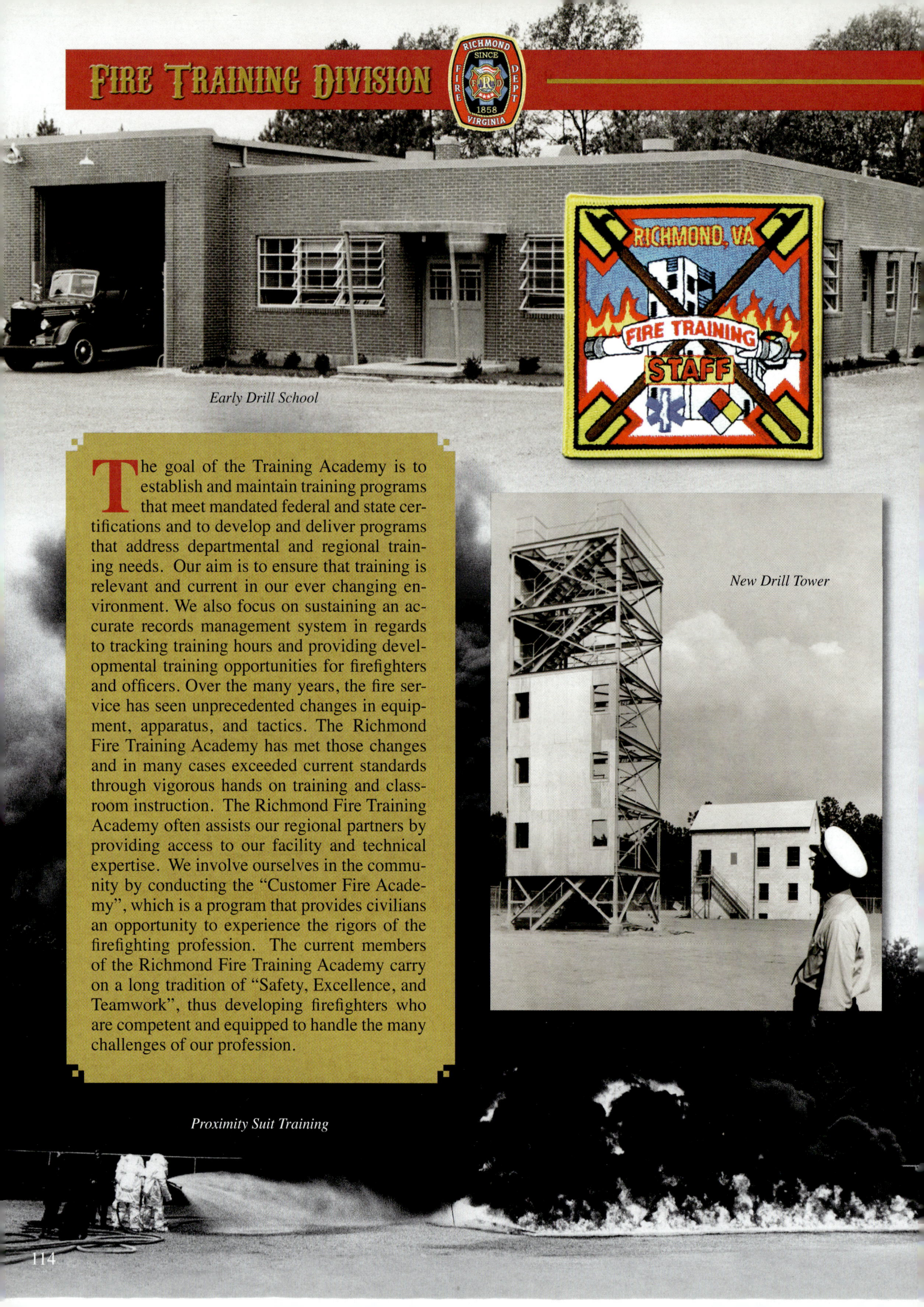

*Early Drill School*

*New Drill Tower*

The goal of the Training Academy is to establish and maintain training programs that meet mandated federal and state certifications and to develop and deliver programs that address departmental and regional training needs. Our aim is to ensure that training is relevant and current in our ever changing environment. We also focus on sustaining an accurate records management system in regards to tracking training hours and providing developmental training opportunities for firefighters and officers. Over the many years, the fire service has seen unprecedented changes in equipment, apparatus, and tactics. The Richmond Fire Training Academy has met those changes and in many cases exceeded current standards through vigorous hands on training and classroom instruction. The Richmond Fire Training Academy often assists our regional partners by providing access to our facility and technical expertise. We involve ourselves in the community by conducting the "Customer Fire Academy", which is a program that provides civilians an opportunity to experience the rigors of the firefighting profession. The current members of the Richmond Fire Training Academy carry on a long tradition of "Safety, Excellence, and Teamwork", thus developing firefighters who are competent and equipped to handle the many challenges of our profession.

*Proximity Suit Training*

# Fire Training Division

*Pit Fire Training in 1968*

*Simulated Basement Fire*

*Learning the New Breathing Apparatus*

115

# COMMUNICATIONS

*Watchman's Rattle Used to Alert Others in the Event of Fire*

*Watchman Thompson*

Since the early days of the ever vigilant watchman, the need to alert people in the event of fire has always been paramount. From the rattle to the alarm bells, and eventually digital media, the ability to summon help in time of need has evolved to meet the demands of a growing population. The men and women assigned to the Division of Emergency Communications field over 1 million telephone calls per year generating more than 35,000 Richmond Fire Department responses. They are responsible for dispatching the resources of the fire department, police, Virginia Power, gas utilities, and other city and state entities, in addition to coordinating mutual aid with surrounding agencies. Currently Emergency Communications is made up of 74 full time, highly trained dispatchers, using state of the art equipment to ensure the proper resources arrive to mitigate any emergency situation.

*First Electric Fire Alarm*

*Fire Alarm Office in City Hall*

118

# COMMUNICATIONS

*1800's Alarm Wagon*

*Box Alarms*

*First Two Way Radio, 1945*

*Signal Office, 1961*

*First Electric Alarm Put in Service*

*Fire Alarm Office*

119

# Communications

*Current Fire Communications located at 3516 N. Hopkins Road*

*Monroe Park Communications Office, Built in 1923*

*1856 Alarm Bell*

*Billy Stevens*

*Bruce Bullington and Pat Ware*

120

# Richmond Fire Department
## Personnel

# Fire Chief

*Robert A. Creecy*

# Deputy Chiefs

*Melvin D. Carter*

*Elmond D. Taylor*

# BATTALION CHIEFS

Lynwood Buchanan III

Warren A. Cersley

David C. Creasy Sr.

Jeffrey G. Currie

Robert L. Duffus

Lawrence E. Glidewell Jr.

Glenn E. Grooms

Ramon D. Hardy Jr.

Joseph Jenkins

David D. Pulliam Jr.

Scott E. Schoenhut

Kent O. Taylor Sr.

Tracy A. Thomas

## CHAPLAIN

Reverend Bruce Gray

123

# Officers

## ABDUS-SABUR – HAGAMAN

| | | | | | |
|---|---|---|---|---|---|
| Sekou A. Abdus-Sabur |  Ross C. E. Anderson |  Keith T. Andes |  William E. Andrews |  Christopher G. Aycock |  Robert S. Baumgardner Jr. |
|  William A. Beatley Jr. |  Rodney R. Berbert |  Timothy S. Brandon |  Alan D. Brooke |  Stephen P. Brown |  David C. Burns |
|  Ludenilo D. Castro Jr. |  Paul F. Chavis |  Chuvalo D. Christian Sr. | 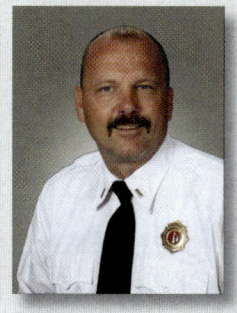 Mark A. Dabrishus |  Brian E. Dalrymple |  Warren G. Davis |
|  William O. Davis |  David F. Doane |  Earl E. Dyer Jr. |  Rodney D. Epps |  Ronald K. Faulconer |  Donald R. Foreman Jr. |
|  Stephen T. Forgette |  Menshian A. George |  Kevin D. Gibson |  William E. Goode III |  Kurt E. Gran |  Robert C. Hagaman |

# HARKNESS – RICHARDSON OFFICERS

John E. Harkness  | Edgar C. Harris Jr.  | Sylvester I. Henderson  | Alfred D. Holmes  | Darl W. Jewell  | Gregory M. Johnson

Walter L. Johnson  | Anthony A. Jones  | Shawn L. Jones  | Kyle L. Kyger 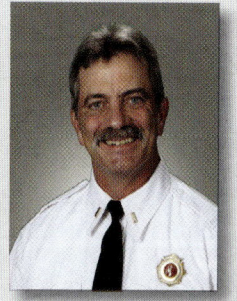 | Bryan Law  | Clarence E. Lewis III

Richard D. Lewis Jr.  | Melvin V. Liverman III 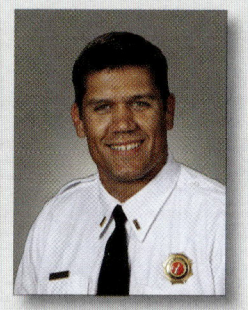 | Bailey C. Martin Jr.  | William M. Martin  | Robin C. McCarter 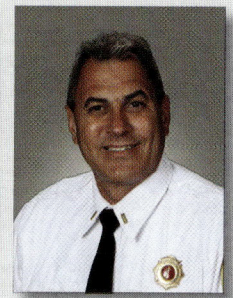 | Terry L. McGirt

Orlando L. Morris  | James E. Nelsen  | Hallie T. Neville  | Raymond N. Neville  | Steven W. Nixon  | Michael A. Oprandy

Patrick J. Peddicord  | Donald K. Polifka Jr.  | Michael W. Powell  | Travis L. Preau  | Mark V. Rada  | Christine Richardson

# Officers

## RICHARDSON – WATKINS

- Stephen B. Richardson
- Harold B. Ring 
- Andre R. Roberts 
- David M. Ross 
- Ricky L. Rosser 
- Melissa A. Russ 
- Don A. Salotti 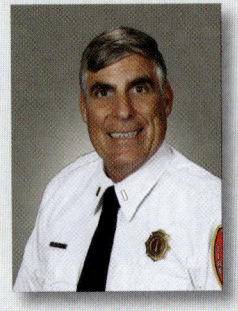
- Patrick M. Schoeffel 
- Donald N. Shelton 
- Gary W. Shortt 
- Carroll E. Smith 
- Claude F. Smith Jr. 
- John P. Spanbauer 
- Melody C. Spivey 
- Kevin T. Spruill 
- Charles U. Stowell Jr. 
- William R. Talley 
- Blake L. Toepke 
- Kenneth L. Townes 
- Brian C. Turnage 
- Keith M. Vida 
- William Vytlacil 
- Mark O. Wagner 
- James W. Walker 
- Tina R. Watkins

## WEST – GITTMAN — OFFICERS

| | | | | | |
|---|---|---|---|---|---|
| Bobby R. West |  Garland W. Weymouth |  Jerry W. Williams |  Sheldon L. Williams |  Fred D. Wright | 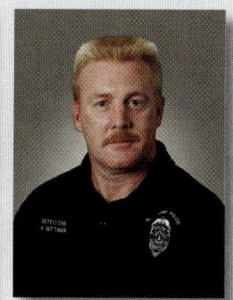 Howard E. Gittman *Detective* |

## AILOR – BRASWELL — FIREFIGHTERS

| | | | | | |
|---|---|---|---|---|---|
| Alexander T. Ailor |  Wesley F. Amos |  Elshod D. Anderson |  Michael S. Anderson |  Dwight E. Andrews |  Kelly R. Andrews |
|  Leonard J. Archer |  Christopher W. Armstrong |  Michael S. Ashby |  Joshua D. Atkins |  Charles M. Barkley |  Antoine S. Bediako |
|  Bell, Mary A. Jr. |  Gregory L. Bembry |  Alvin L. Berry Sr. |  James P. Bohn |  Jeffry P. Bohn |  Michael P. Braswell |

127

# FireFighters — BRAWAND – COUSINS

| | | |
|---|---|---|
| Mark A. Brawand |  Charles W. Bridgers |  George R. Bridgers Jr. |
|  Thomas E. Brockenbrough |  William S. Brooks |  Eric R. Brown |
|  Kenneth L. Brown |  Roderick S. Brown |  Antonio R. Bullock |
|  William B. Bullock |  Michael A. Burrell |  Darryl E. Burton |
|  Timothy M. Butler |  Bonnie M. Cabello |  Dwayne A. Carter |
|  Melvin L. Cash Jr. |  Andrew W. Cersley |  Mark A. Chase |
|  Thomas A. Chenault Jr. | 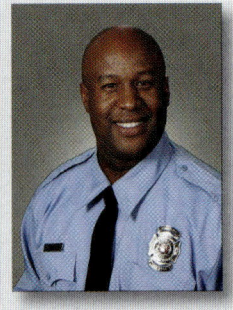 Jonathan E. Clarke |  William S. Clements Jr. |
|  Douglas G. Cogar |  Keith W. Coleman |  Shawn I. Coleman |
|  Rodney J. Coles |  Christopher L. Conley |  Jerry P. Conwell |
|  James E. Conyers |  Hampton L. Couser |  Linwood H. Cousins Jr. |

# COZZIE – GORDON

## FIREFIGHTERS

Christopher J. Cozzie  | Michael W. Crabtree  | Michael R. Crawley Sr.  | Jennifer J. Curran  | Steven M. Curry  | Chuck L. Davis

Isaiah P. Davis Jr.  | Raymond E. Davis  | Dennis D. Day  | George A. Dean Jr.  | Joel E. Dodson Jr.  | Daniel T. Dolan

James R. Duncan  | Ronald L. Edwards  | Ronald L. Edwards Jr.  | Sanford M. Edwards Jr.  | Bryan P. Elrod  | Jennifer A. Elrod

Malcolm J. Epps Jr.  | Robert L. Ervin  | William G. Eudailey Jr.  | Alex J. Farber  | Chris A. Fitzgerald  | Keith M. Fleming

Rodney I. Fleming  | James E. Flippin Jr.  | Jamila A. Flowers  | Walter Funn  | Carlin E. Gibson 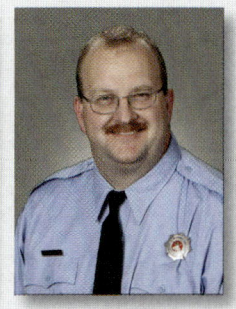 | Jason R. Gordon

# FireFighters

## GOUGH – HUDGINS

| | | | | | |
|---|---|---|---|---|---|
| James T. Gough Jr. |  Jerry D. Gowen |  Bernard Graham |  Samuel M. Graham Jr. |  Robert E. Gray |  Dariel Green |
|  David W. Griffin |  Erik M. Grooms |  Michelle L. Haga |  Ronald R. Hagen |  Charles J. Haines |  Steven E. Hall Jr. |
|  Thomas W. Hamm |  Kenna T. Harkley |  Michael G. Harman Jr. |  Andre L. Harris |  Kevin W. Harris |  Stacey A. Harris |
|  Ward M. Harris Jr. |  William W. Harris |  Kevin Harrison Jr. |  Martin C. Hart |  John D. Heller |  James E. Herbin Jr. |
|  David C. Hicks |  Christopher W. Hoover |  Dion T. Horton |  Kevin E. House |  Arlington L. Huband Jr. |  Alvis J. Hudgins |

# IRWIN – MARY

## FIREFIGHTERS

| | | | | | |
|---|---|---|---|---|---|
| Mark D. Irwin |  Erik R. James |  Christopher C. Jefferson |  Anthony G. Johnson Sr. |  Durrell R. Johnson |  James V. Johnson |
|  Lenhard R. Johnson |  Ronnie P. Jones |  William C. Jones Jr. |  Erdal Karabulut |  Samad A. Khabir |  Kevin A. Knight |
|  Larry D. Knight |  Pope J. Kofie |  John S. Kuper III |  Sean M. Labadie |  Courtland A. Lambert Jr. |  Jeffrey L. Lawson |
|  John W. Lawson |  Phillips S. Ledbetter |  Clifton Lee |  Clinton M. Lewis |  Gary R. Lewis Jr. |  Donnie L. Little |
|  David M. Loving |  John T. Lukhard |  Robert T. Maass |  William C. Mack |  Jason P. Martin |  Joseph A. Mary |

# FireFighters

## MARZIALE – NEVILLE

| | | | | | |
|---|---|---|---|---|---|
| Peter J. Marziale |  Kouri R. Mayhew |  James A. McCain |  George L. McCall Jr. |  Phillip A. McCarter |  William J. McCarthy |
|  William B. McCarty |  Lupe M. McCloud |  Michael E. McCormick | 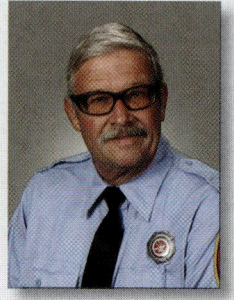 William A. McFarland |  Shawn P. McGovern |  Jack R. McIntyre |
|  Francis J. McKearin III |  John J. Melchek |  Adam C. Mesco |  Eric R. Mesco |  Leo A. Mesco Jr. |  Charles P. Mezera |
|  Terry L. Milby |  Michael G. Miller |  Arthur R. Minter Jr. |  Christopher J. Moore |  Jody T. Moore |  Marshall P. Moran |
|  Gregory K. Mundie |  Benjamin P. Murray |  Michael W. Murrin |  Roger R. Myers Jr. |  Reginold R. Nelson |  Laura P. Neville |

# NEWCOMB – RYALS

## FireFighters

| | | | | | |
|---|---|---|---|---|---|
| Wayne P. Newcomb |  Richard A. Nunnally Jr. |  Daniel T. Owens | 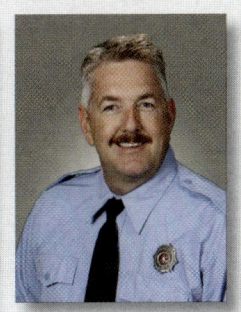 Mark W. Owens |  Nathan C. Oyler |  Robert W. Parker |
|  D'Jalmar A. Perry |  Ronald R. Perry |  Korey L. Pettiford |  Lawrence E. Plaskett Jr. | 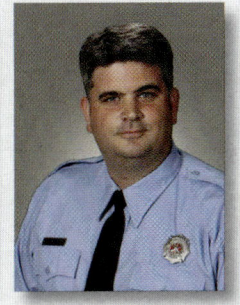 Craig W. Pollard |  Wilton V. Portwood |
|  Michael L. Possanza |  Jamie L. Potter |  Timothy W. Pratt | 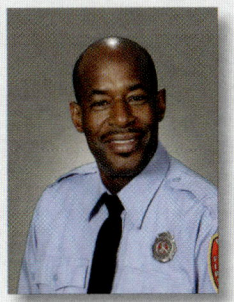 Kennard Pritchett |  Steven W. Ragsdale |  James C. Reamey |
|  Anthony M. Rice |  Brian K. Rice |  William M. Rice |  William J. Riddell |  Sean P. Riley |  Darnell J. Rippy |
|  Robert L. Rivers Jr. |  Kimberly M. Roberts |  Bruce D. Robertson |  Melvin L. Ruffin |  David H. Runion |  Mark K. Ryals |

# FIREFIGHTERS

## RYAN – STEVENS

Stephen J. Ryan  | Jabari O. Salim  | Melvin D. Satchell  | Lloyd D. Satterwhite  | Jay S. Scales Sr.  | Jay S. Scales Jr.

Joseph R. Schmidt  | Douglas S. Seal  | James L. Seay Jr.  | Clephos Sessions Sr.  | Floyd N. Sessions Sr.  | Charles K. Shears

Donald Shires  | Ronald A. Short  | William A. Shulleeta  | Joseph J. Signorelli  | Marco R. Siguenza  | Patrick J. Simon

Otis L. Sims  | Stratford L. Slater Jr.  | Barry G. Smith  | Michael E. Smith Jr.  | Shaundell L. Smith  | William T. Smith

Christopher W. Spencer  | William T. Spindle III  | Rodney Spruill  | Terrence T. Squire  | Michael J. Stallings  | Scott D. Stevens

# STEVENSON – WASHINGTON        FireFighters

| | | | | | | |
|---|---|---|---|---|---|---|
| Dewarren K. Stevenson |  Adam M. Stewart |  Patrick M. Stewart |  Elton F. Stinson |  Edward B. Stokes |  Charles U. Stowell III |
|  Christopher W. Stowell |  Kellie Andes Stowell |  Christopher Strybing |  George Taylor III |  Stewart A. Thiel |  Michael L. Throckmorton |
|  Lee A. Todd |  John A. Trent |  Charles C. Trimble |  Alonzo E. Trimiew Sr. |  James C. Turner |  Steven L. Turpin |
|  Wayne P. Tyler |  James E. Verlander |  Paul M. VonMille |  Chadwick S. Waddy |  Daniel S. Waldron |  Rodger W. Walker |
|  Robert W. Wall |  Ronald N. Walton |  Linwood L. Waltrip II |  William K. Ware |  Norman E. Washington |  Ronald T. Washington Sr. |

135

# FireFighters

## WATERS – BAILEY

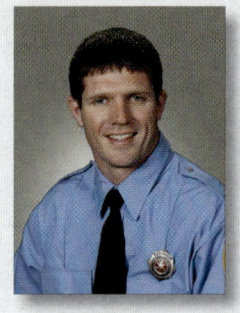

| | | | | | |
|---|---|---|---|---|---|
| Brion N. Waters |  Mark W. Watkins |  Michael E. Watson |  Larry F. Watts |  Steven K. Wegner |  Anthony L. Wells |
|  Christopher D. Wells |  Kenneth W. West Sr. |  Joseph D. White |  Shaun T. Whiteley |  Kevin N. Whitlock |  Barry M. Wilkerson |
| 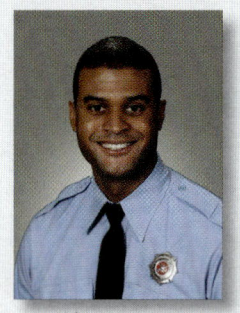 Michael T. Wilkins |  Gui J. Williams |  John M. Williams |  Terrance I. Williams |  Thelburt A. Williams |  Thomas L. Williams |
| |  Tyrelle C. Williams |  Steven W. Williamson |  Marlon R. Winston |  Robert C. Witherspoon | |
| |  Everett B. Wood |  David L. Wright Sr. |  Neale P. Wright | 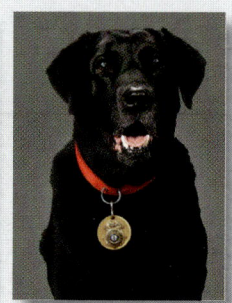 Bailey | |

136

## BURROUGHS – WILSON-CHO

## Administrative Staff

Marilyn B. Burroughs

Joy C. Haynesworth

Nancy Hall

Theresa M. Hunter

Tangela U. Innis

Mini G. Menon

Christopher A. Morris

Mary Beth Niver

Christina H. Smith

Kimberly Wilson-Cho

# RETIREES

## ACORS – WOODCOCK

Russell G. Acors III
BC Hanover County FD

Nelson P. Boykin
Lieutenant

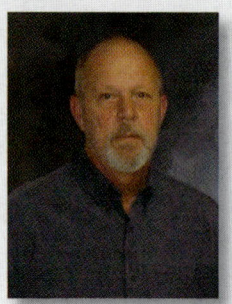

Steven Brandon
Firefighter

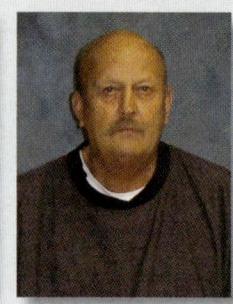

Thomas Brandon
Firefighter

William Bullock
Firefighter

Richard E. Burch Jr.,
Chief of Roanoke Co. FD

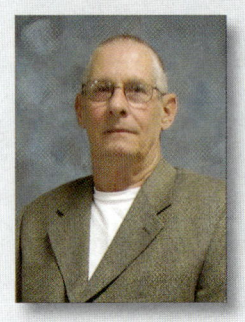

Frank P. Castelvecchi
Firefighter

Warren O. Christian
Firefighter

Rondal F. Coffey
Firefighter

M. Wayne Dawson
Firefighter

Richard E. Gregory
Firefighter

James F. Gross
Firefighter

Carl R. Hansen
Firefighter

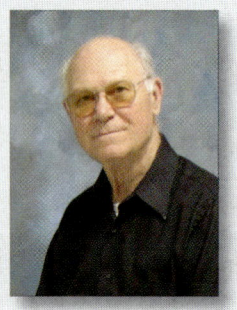

John E. Harrell
Lieutenant

John E. Hinant
Captain

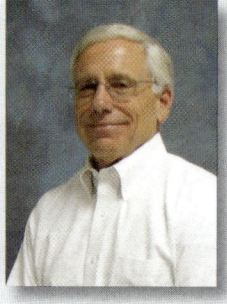

Thomas L. Herman
Firefighter

Paul A. Holley
Firefighter

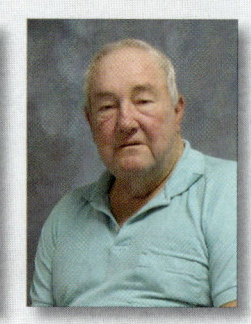

Luther H. Jennings
Firefighter

William E. Jones
BC Hanover County FD

Bobby E. Lambert
Firefighter

Wallace H. Lawrence Jr.
Assistant Fire Chief

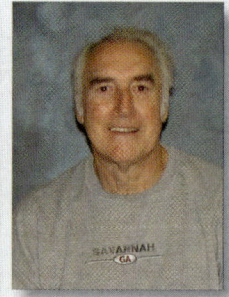

Julian E. Madison
Battalion Chief

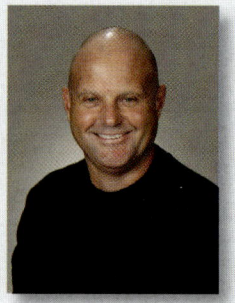

Douglas D. Nicholson
Firefighter

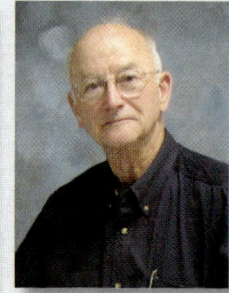

William C. Poole
Lieutenant

Bland E. Shaughnessy
Assistant Fire Chief

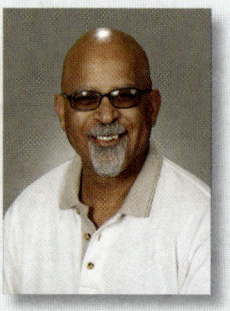

Warren A. Smith
Lieutenant

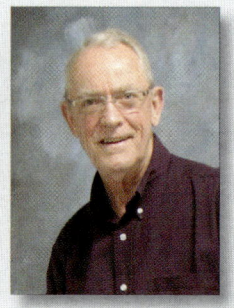

Ross A. Southers Jr.
Firefighter

Reginald K. Sterling
Firefighter

Joan Draucker Williams
Fire Chief's Secretary

Robert A. Woodcock
Lieutenant

# STATION LIFE

*Late Evening Relaxation*

*Sliding the Pole*

*Watch Desk*

*Cleaning the Rig*

The neighborhood firehouse is much more than a work place. In early times the local firehouse was a gathering place for citizens and civic leaders as well. A focal point of the community, the local firehouse served as the safe place that people within the community knew they could always rely on for assistance no matter what the need. The needs were not always emergencies. Sometimes folks would come for directions or just friendly conversation to catch up on current events. Children would visit in hopes of an opportunity to sit on the shiny fire truck and maybe ring the bell a time or two. Regardless of the nature of the visit, people knew that the firefighters would always oblige them with assistance in any way they could without complaint or hesitation. The firefighters of the day took great pride in the appearance of their house and equipment. Hours spent polishing chrome, washing, and waxing until the truck shined like a new penny. The truck then would be parked in front of the fire house for all to see the fruits of their labor. Much time was also spent sitting in front of the station engaged in stories about the "big one," or the "coldest one", or the pranks that had been played on the unsuspecting rookie fireman paying his dues. As tales are told and laughs are shared, a bond is formed, and that bond grows stronger with each passing day. For beneath the surface of this great profession lies a brotherhood that brings firefighters from all over the world together and while it cannot be fully understood by the general public, it beats in the hearts of the men and women who serve. Over the years this great profession has witnessed many changes, yet the traditions of the firehouse have remained mostly intact. Today's firefighters can still be found sharing a morning pot of coffee, discussing current events, mopping floors, washing dishes, cleaning the rig, or training on their craft, ever vigilant for the next alarm that will call them into harms way. As the job begins and station life is put on hold, silently, they share the hope that all will go home safe at shifts end.

# Station Life

*Engine 1 Mascot*

*Driver Checks*

*Packing the Hose*

*House Watch*

*Hydrant Maintenance*

*Morning Coffee*

140

# STATION LIFE

*Chow Time*

*Down Time*

*Keeping Them Ready*

*Spanish Class*

*Meetings with the Chief*

*Team Building*

# NOTABLE EVENTS

## RICHMOND, VA, FIRE DECEMBER 1811

About the first of the following January, news of a great calamity at Richmond, Virginia reached Providence. The theatre was destroyed by fire and many lives were lost. From some mismanagement of the lights, the scenery was ignited. The flames spread with rapidity, and the cry of "Fire!" rang through the house. The occupants of the pit and gallery at once made their escape, but those in the boxes were not so fortunate. The entrance to the hall was narrow and accessed by a winding passage. The struggle to gain egress was so great that it became blocked. All present might have escaped, if they had jumped into the pit, but no one thought of that expedient. They became panic-stricken. The smoke blinded them, and terrified by the progress of the flames. They became powerless, and were either trodden under foot or perished in the raging fire. Seventy-one persons, including the governor of the State, lost their lives in this disaster.

The next day all places of business in Richmond were closed. A law was passed prohibiting amusements of every kind for the term of four months. Citizens wore mourning attire for a month. At Washington, the representatives of the several states assumed the customary badges of grief, and all amusements were suspended. This sad occurrence created a deep sensation throughout the country, and in Providence it produced an unusual gloom and depression. (*History of the Providence Stage, 1762-1891, page 50*)

## RICHMOND, VA, CHURCH FIRE, APRIL 1856

**DESTRUCTIVE TO FIRE IN RICHMOND, VA, CHURCH BURNED** – Yesterday morning, about 1 o'clock, the large frame building on Eighteenth Street, between Franklin and Grace, occupied by Mr. O. A. Francis as a carriage factory, was set on fire, and, the timber being very dry and combustible, the flames spread with such rapidity that three boys who slept in the shop barely had time to escape in their nightclothes. Before the firemen could get their apparatus in operation the edifice was wrapped in a sheet of flames, which speedily communicated with Messrs. Rowe & Meredith's wheelwright and blacksmith shop, which was also properly destroyed. While these buildings were in flames, a stiff south breeze sprang up, and drove myriads of sparks and floating coals upon Christ Church, on Grace Street. The firemen seeing the danger in which this edifice stood, directed their energies to its preservation, but without effect, for the roof took fire, and the flames speedily wound themselves around the cupola, which was built of heart timber and burning through it, the falling sparks fired the church inside, sending forth such intense heat that it was impossible for the firemen to approach it. In the meantime the roof of Mr. Duke's stable took fire in several places, and threatened to fire the buildings on the opposite side of the street, but the firemen succeeded in subduing the fire at this point, after having extinguished the burning roof of Seabrook's warehouse, which caught fire several times, saving Mr. Mangum's residence adjoining the church, preventing the destruction of Mr. Duke's stable, and protecting a large number of frame buildings in the neighborhood.

Mr. Francis has lost $4,000 or £5,000 in stock and ready-made work, upon which he had no insurance. All the journeymen lost their tools. Messrs. Rowe & Meredith have lost about $500; no insurance. Mr. Thomas Duke's loss is about $200; no insurance. The Trustees of Christ Church had a small insurance in the Mutual Office, but as the organ, books and everything else but the walls were destroyed, the loss cannot fall short of $6,000. (*From the Richmond Dispatch*)

## RICHMOND, VA, FIRE, SEPTEMBER 1869

**RICHMOND, Va., Sept. 6.---**A fire broke out tonight on Cary Street, near Fourteenth, completely destroying the following premises: JOHNSON, HARWOOD & ESTES' lumber-yard; G. W. CRANDALL & CO.'s planing mill; BOYLE & GAMBLE, saw works; GORSDORF'S file factory, and MASSIE & HARVEY'S grocery and liquor store. The following buildings took fire, but were saved from destruction: BOARD & HIRSCH'S commission-house; CHARLES HOWARD'S commission-house; SLOAT & ADDINGTON'S machine factory, and STARR, WILSON & FOSTER'S warehouse. The loss will probably reach $200,000. (*The New York Times, New York, NY 7 Sept 1869*)

## RICHMOND, VA, COURT ROOM FLOOR COLLAPSE, APRIL 1870

A terrible calamity occurred here this morning. The floor of the Court of Appeals, in the State Capitol, gave way and precipitated the hundreds therein assembled to hear the decision in the Mayoralty case of Ellison and Cahoon, upon the Conservative caucus then sitting in the Hall of the House of Delegates below. It is impossible to ascertain the extent of the injuries at this hour.

Among the killed are P. H. Aylett, a distinguished lawyer; Dr. J. B. Brock, reporter for the Enquirer and Examiner; Samuel Eaton, Clerk of Mayor Cahoon; Captain William A. Charters, Chief of the Fire Department; N. P. Howard, a lawyer; Ash Levy, a Richmond merchant; Charles Watson, of the Danville Railroad; Hugh Hutcheson, Lewis N. Webb. of this city; Wheeler Schofield, brother of General Schofield; R. H. Maury, Jr., Senator Bland (colored), and Powhattan Roberts.

It is supposed that twenty members of the State Legislature are killed or wounded. The Judges of the Court of Appeals all escaped unhurt. Ex-Governor Wells was badly injured. L. H. Chandler, counsel for Cahoon in the Mayoralty case, was injured. James Mason and Judge Meredith, counsel for Ellison, were also badly hurt.

About two hundred persons were hurt by the accident. The greatest excitement prevails, and hundreds of persons in the Capitol Square are weeping and wailing as the dead and dying are brought out of the building. Governor Walker escaped unhurt, though on the floor of the Court room at the time. Directly after the disaster occurred the fire alarm was used to give notice, and the hook and ladder companies of the city repaired at once to the scene. A cordon of police was drawn around the building, and the ladders were thrown up to the windows. For three hours the scene was full of horror. Minute after minute there appeared, swung out by a rope tied around the middle, the body of some popular favorite, who after being swung on to the shoulders of one of the fire brigade were brought down the ladder into the green of the public Park, where it was instantly surrounded by two or three thousand of those who had gathered to recognize the slain. The Park was filled with anxious, weeping women and anxious men until two o'clock, when the last victim was drawn from the building. (*The Philadelphia Inquirer, Philadelphia PA 28 Apr 1870*)

## RICHMOND, VA FIRE, MARCH 26, 1882

**RICHMOND, VA., March 26.** – One of the most destructive conflagrations which ever visited this city , and second only to that which destroyed the business portion on its evacuation by the Confederate Army in April 1865, occurred here today, resulting in a great destruction of property, the loss of one life, and several minor casualties. A number of poor people are deprived of their homes and household goods and the traveling public inconve-

# NOTABLE EVENTS

nienced by the loss of the main bridge connecting the northern and southern systems of railway crossing the James River at this point. At 12:30 today an employee of the Richmond and Petersburg Railroad Company discovered a small blaze near the southern end of the company's long bridge over the James River, and immediately started to give an alarm. In a few minutes a portion of the Fire Department was responding, but by the time it arrived at the fire, aided by a heavy gale from the south-west, had made such a rapid progress that the bridge was wrapped in flames and in less than half an hour the whole structure fell a mass of ruins, into the river, leaving nothing standing but the granite piers upon which the bridge was built and which are placed at interval across the river. The bridge was originally built in 18[??], and was destroyed by fire at the time of the evacuation of Richmond and rebuilt in 1866. It was a "Howe truss" structure of the old style, with a frame trunk about 18 feet deep, upon which the track was laid. To the combustible nature of the bridge, combined with the high wind, was due its swift destruction. When the flames reached the Richmond end of the bridge they immediately seized upon the large four-story brick tobacco factory of T. M. Rutherford & Co., which also quickly fell victim. From that point the fire continued to spread with frightful rapidity, attacking and laying in ashes in quick succession the large brick tobacco factories of R. A. Patterson & Co., T. C. Williams & Co., the three tobacco stemmeries of J. A. Huchinson, two stemmeries of C. R. and F. D. Barksdale, the stemmery of Aborn & Edwards, the Vulcan Ironworks, operated by Bruce & Archer; 20 tenements houses, occupied by poor people; about 300 feet of trestle-work connecting the Tredegar Iron-works with the Richmond and Petersburg Railroad, 10 new freight cars, belonging to the Tredegar Company; T. P. Smith's grist mill, a number of other minor buildings, and a quantity of coal and lumber at the southern or Manchester end of the bridge. The Virginia Mining and Manufacturing Company's Kaoline works were also destroyed. When it became evident that the bridge was in imminent danger, second and third fire alarms were sounded and the whole Fire Department was called out, but the efforts of the firemen to check the flames were entirely futile, fighting, as they were obliged to, against the fierce winds, which, driving the flames, cinders, and smoke into their faces, forced them back foot by foot. At 1:45 P. M., Mayor Carrington telegraphed to Washington for assistance from the Fire Department of that city, but later, when the fire was finally under control, another telegram was sent to Washington to that effect. The Washington department had responded promptly and had placed several engines on a special train when informed that their services were not needed. The fire occurred at about the time the churches were being dismissed, and the alarm being immediately given by every fire apparatus and hall in the city notification of the calamity spread with rapidity, and in a short time the hills and house – tons and every elevation affording a place of view were densely thronged with old and young, white and colored. The heavy wind added more than ordinary vitality to the flames and carried large pieces of burning cinders for long distances, which in some cases set fire to distant roofs. (*New York Times, New York, NY 27 Mar 1882*)

## RICHMOND, VA, THREE FIREMEN KILLED, OCTOBER 10, 1915

Falling brick walls, following a fire which destroyed Crenshaw's warehouse in Shockoe Slip and tobacco and other stock valued at more than $500,000, caused the death of three members of the city fire department today. The dead are: CAPT. RICHARD M. NORMENT, C.L. ATKINSON, and W.R. ODELL, members of No. 1 Fire Company.

After the fire was practically under control the firemen ventured too near one of the walls of the Crenshaw warehouse. It fell with a fearful crash. Captain Norment was instantly killed, while Atkinson and Odell were crushed so badly that death occurred a few hours after they were rescued by the comrades. A. K. Davenport and D.D.C. Johnson were injured and are in a serious condition.

*C & O Fire, 1917*

# NOTABLE EVENTS

*Jurgens Fire Sunday March 13th. 1921*

*No. 6 Co.*

The fire was discovered shortly after 1 o'clock this morning the Crenshaw warehouse. Thousands of pounds of tobacco, stored there for shipment to Italy, were lost. Other buildings burned were those of F.V. Gunn & Co., the Federal Sugar Refining Company and the R.A. Canthorne Paper Company.

A strong wind was blowing and only by the hard work of the entire city fire department was the blaze confined to the square within which it started. (*The Sun, Baltimore, MD 11 Oct 1915*)

## RICHMOND, VA. LEXINGTON HOTEL FIRE, FEBRUARY 27, 1922

"Evidence of gross negligence, incompetence and a want of proper regard for the safety and lives of both guests and employees," is the finding of the special grand jury, after an investigation into the Lexington hotel fire disaster which, February 7, took a toll of 12 lives and sent many persons pitifully injured to hospitals, as submitted late this afternoon to Judge D. C. Richardson, of Hustings court.

No criminal violation of the law was found by the jury, it reported. The following significant statement is used in the findings:

"The hotel register is headed 'the New Lexington hotel,' a delusion and a snare, often used to catch trade and fool the unwary traveler. A coat of paint or a little wall paper does not make a new hotel out of an old shack, and tends to extend the use of such hotels long years after they should be demolished. Such naming is false and should be prevented by law."

Judge Richardson will forward the reports to Mayor George Ainslie, with the request that he communicate with city council as to its recommendations for safeguarding hotel guests in the future. (*The Miami Herald, Miami, FL 28 Feb 1922*)

*THE RICHMOND NEWS LEADER*
**EX-GOVERNOR PRICE'S WIDOW, SEN. WEAVER, 4 OTHERS DEAD, 20 HURT IN JEFFERSON FIRE**

*Jefferson Hotel Fire, 1944*

*Dominion Tire, 1967*

144

## Notable Events

*Eastern Sleep Mattress Company, 1979*

*FF Cersley at Little Oil Fire*

*Little Oil Storage Tank Fire, 1976*

*Little Oil Aftermath*

*Standard Paper Fire*

145

# Notable Events

*Crew Working at Star Warehouse Fire, July 11, 1979*

*Sonoco on Commerce Road, 2004*

*St. James Church, July 13, 1994*

*VCU, Rear View on Fire, 2004*

*VCU at Street Level, 2004*

## NOTABLE EVENTS

*North Side, 2008*

*Arbors Seniors' Community Fire, 2004*

*The Arbors Fire Aftermath, 2004*

*3rd Alarm on Clay Street, August 2008*

*1017 Hioaks Apartments Fire Aftermath, 2009*

# Man's Best Friend

Lt. Weymouth pulls one out on Spruance Street.

Stokes, Walker, and Rivers work for the save.

Pet Mask Applied

A Grateful Friend!

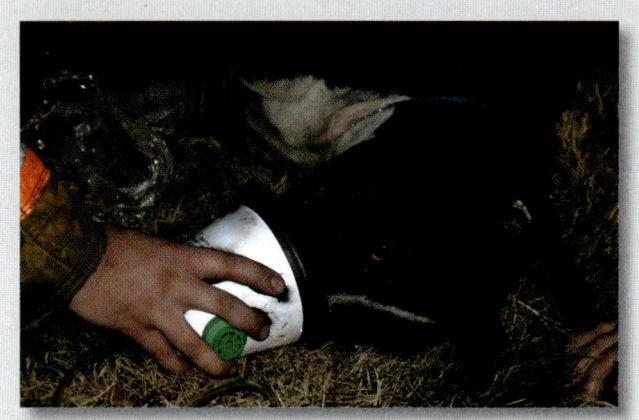

Conrad Street

Harkness on Wise Sreet - Four Puppies Saved!

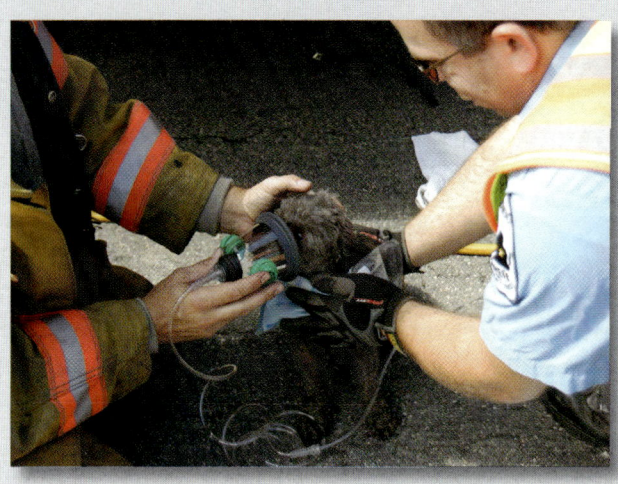

Application of the Pet Resuscitation Mask

148

# MDA & JERRY'S KIDS

For many years, firefighters from all over the United States and Canada have championed the cause of helping to raise dollars in support of the Muscular Dystrophy Association, and the firefighters of the City of Richmond are no exception. Each year in August the fight expands and the focus is on helping "Jerry's Kids". Firefighters on and off duty take to the streets and intersections with boots in hand ready to raise the important dollars needed to find a cure for this terrible neuro-muscular condition. To date, the selfless members of the Richmond Fire Department have raised in excess of a half a million dollars towards this cause. In addition, volunteers attend MDA Summer Camp in June where children with Muscular Dystrophy are treated to petting zoo's, horse and cart rides, fun, and entertainment. This brief time during the summer does wonders for the hope and morale of the children who attend. Anyone who has ever experienced the joy in the eyes of these brave children, who harbor such serious ailments, can attest that they are in fact the true heroes and that the race to find a cure is paramount. Each year on Labor Day we bare witness to the plight of these little angels through the Jerry Lewis MDA Telethon and each year the request is simple: One Dollar More. That is the battle cry and each year we rise to meet that challenge. No matter what hurdles we may face, Richmond Firefighters will continue to fight for those who cannot fight for themselves in the true nature of our profession.

*Early MDA Collection Efforts*

*FF Lynn Archer*

*MDA Summer Camp Cart Rides*

*Collecting Off Duty*

*Built with Love by Rescue 1 and Quint 1*

*Collecting for a Cure*

*Miles of Smiles*

# INDEX

## A

**Abdus-Sabur**, Sekou A. 124
**Aborn** 143
**Acors**, Russell G. III 138
**Ailor**, Alexander T. 127
**Ainslie**, George 16, 144
**Amos**, Wesley F. 127
**Anderson**, Elshod D. 127, Michael S. 127, Ross C. E. 124
**Andes**, Keith T. 124
**Andrews**, Dwight E. 127, Kelly R. 127, William 107, 124
**Archer** 143, L. 111, Leonard J. 127, Lynn 149
**Armstrong**, Christopher W. 127
**Ashby**, Michael S. 127
**Atkins**, Joshua D. 127
**Atkinson**, C. L. 10, 143
**Aycock**, Christopher G. 124
**Aylett**, P. H. 142

## B

**Bailey** 112, 136
**Barkley**, Charles M. 127
**Barksdale**, C. R. 143, F. D. 143
**Barnes**, Lewis L. 16, 21
**Baumgardner**, Rob 7, Robert S. Jr. 124
**Beatley**, William A. Jr. 7, 117, 124
**Bediako**, Antoine S. 127
**Belle**, Charles L. 59, 61
**Bembry**, Gregory L. 127
**Bendle**, E. L. Jr. 11
**Berbert**, Rodney R. 124
**Berry**, Alvin L. Sr. 127
**Bibb**, E. R. 11
**Blake**, Oscar 59, 60, 61
**Bland** 142
**Bohn**, James P. 127, Jeffry P. 127
**Bosher**, James 16, Lewis 16
**Bottoms**, H. C. 11
**Boykin**, Nelson P. 138
**Brandon**, Steven 138, Thomas 138, Timothy S. 124
**Braswell**, Michael P. 127
**Brawand**, Mark A. 128
**Bridgers**, Charles 7, 128, George 7, 128
**Brockenbrough**, Thomas E. 128
**Brock**, J. B. 142
**Brooke**, Alan D. 124
**Brooks**, William S. 128
**Brown** 113, Eric R. 128, Herman 61, Kenneth L. 128, Roderick S. 128, S. 111, Stephen P. 124, William E. 59
**Bruce** 143
**Buchanan**, Lynwood III 123
**Buckner**, J. W. 12
**Bullington**, Bruce 120
**Bullock**, Antonio R. 128, William 128, 138
**Burch**, Richard E. Jr. 138
**Burns**, David 7, 124
**Burrell**, Michael A. 128
**Burroughs**, Marilyn B. 137
**Burton**, Darryl E. 128
**Butler**, Timothy M. 128
**Byrd**, William 19

## C

**Cabello**, Bonnie M. 128
**Canthorne**, R.A. 144
**Carrington** 143
**Carroll**, E. R. Jr. 11
**Carter**, Dwayne A. 128, Melvin D. 122
**Cash**, Melvin 7, 128
**Castelvecchi**, Frank P. 138
**Castro**, Ludenilo D. Jr. 124
**Cersley**, Andrew W. 128, Warren A. 123
**Chandler**, L. H. 142
**Charters**, William A. 16, 142
**Chase**, Mark A. 128
**Chavis**, Paul F. 124
**Chenault**, T. 111, Thomas A. Jr. 128
**Christian**, Chuvalo D. Sr. 124, Warren O. 138
**Clarke**, Jonathan E. 128
**Clements**, William S. Jr. 128
**Coffey**, Rondal F. 138
**Cogar**, Douglas G. 128
**Coleman**, Keith W. 128, Shawn I. 128
**Coles**, Rodney J. 128
**Conley**, Christopher L. 128
**Conwell**, Jerry P. 128
**Conyers**, James E. 128
**Cosby**, Clarence 10
**Cotton**, C. A. 11
**Couser**, Hampton L. 128
**Cousins**, Linwood H. Jr. 128
**Cozzie**, Christopher J. 129
**Crabtree**, Michael W. 129
**Crawley**, Michael R. Sr. 129
**Creasy**, A. N. 10, David C. Sr. 111, 123
**Creecy**, Robert 14, 18, 111, 112, 122
**Curran**, Jennifer J. 129
**Currie** 107, Jeffrey G. 123
**Curry**, Steven M. 129

## D

**Dabrishus**, Mark A. 124
**Dalrymple**, Brian E. 124
**Davenport**, A. K. 143
**Davis**, Chuck L. 129, Isaiah P. Jr. 129, Raymond E. 129, Warren G. 124, William O. 124
**Dawson**, M. Wayne 138
**Day**, Dennis D. 129
**Dean**, George A. Jr. 129
**Doane**, David F. 124
**Dodson**, Joel E. Jr. 129
**Dolan**, Daniel T. 129
**Duffus**, Robert L. 123
**Duke**, Thomas 142
**Duncan**, James R. 129
**Dyer**, Earl E. Jr. 124

## E

**Eaton**, Samuel 142
**Edwards** 143, Ronald L. Sr. 129, Ronald L. Jr. 7, 129, Sanford M. Jr. 129
**Ellison** 142
**Elrod**, Bryan P. 129, Jennifer A. 129
**Emerson**, B. E. Jr. 12. Bernard 13
**Epps**, Malcolm J. Jr. 129, Rodney D. 124
**Ervin**, Robert L. 129
**Eudailey**, William G. Jr. 129
**Evans**, D. P. 11, Douglas P. 59, 61

## F

**Farber**, Alex J. 129
**Faulconer**, Ronald K. 124
**Finnegan**, John F. 7, John F. Jr. 17, 29, 105, John F. Sr. 17
**Fitzgerald**, Chris A. 129
**Fleming**, Keith M. 129, Rodney I. 129
**Flippin**, James E. Jr. 129
**Flowers**, Jamila A. 129
**Foreman**, Donald R. Jr. 124
**Forgette**, Stephen T. 124
**Francis**, O. A. 142
**Friend**, Roscoe W. 61
**Fry**, Hugh W. 16, John J. 16, 21
**Funn**, Walter 129
**Fuqua**, Arthur L. 16

## G

**Galliher**, J. B. 10, 25
**George**, Menshian A. 124
**Gibson**, Carlin E. 129, J. S. 11, Kevin D. 124
**Gittman**, H. 111, Howard E. 127
**Glidewell**, Lawrence E. Jr. 123
**Goode**, William E. III 124
**Gordon**, Jason R. 129
**Gough**, James T. Jr. 130
**Gowen**, Jerry D. 130
**Graham**, Bernard 130
**Graham**, Samuel M. Jr. 130
**Gran**, Kurt E. 124
**Gray**, Bruce 123, Robert E. 130
**Green**, Dariel 130
**Gregory**, Richard E. 138
**Griffin**, David W. 130, M. 12, Marvin 13
**Griggs**, Walter S. Jr. 7
**Grooms**, Erik M. 130, Glenn E. 123
**Gross**, James F. 138
**Gunn**, F.V. 144
**Guthrie**, J. R. 10, 25

## H

**Haga**, Michelle L. 130
**Hagaman**, Robert C. 124
**Hagen**, Ronald R. 130
**Haines**, Charles J. 130
**Hall**, Jerry 13, J.W. 12, Nancy 137, Steven E. Jr. 130
**Hamm**, Thomas W. 130
**Hansen**, Carl R. 138
**Hardy**, Ramon D. Jr. 123
**Harkley**, Kenna T. 130
**Harkness** 148, John E. 125
**Harman**, Michael G. Jr. 130
**Harrell**, John E. 138
**Harris**, Andre L. 130, Billy 13, B. W. 12, Edgar C. Jr. 125, Kevin W. 130, Stacey A. 130, Ward M. Jr. 130, William W. 130
**Harrison**, Kevin Jr. 130
**Hart**, Martin C. 130
**Harthorne** 19
**Haynesworth**, Joy C. 105, 137
**Heinecke**, Adolph 25
**Heller**, John D. 130
**Henderson**, Sylvester I. 125
**Herbin**, James E. Jr. 130
**Herman**, Thomas 6, 7, 138
**Hicks**, Barbara 29, David C. 130, Harvey S. 11, 59, 60, 61
**Hill**, H. O. 11
**Hinant**, John 6, 7, 138
**Holley**, Paul A. 138
**Holmes**, Alfred D. 125
**Hoover**, Christopher W. 130
**Horton** 108, Dion T. 130
**House**, Kevin E. 130
**Howard**, N. P. 142
**Huband**, Arlington L. Jr. 130
**Huchinson**, J. A. 143
**Hudgins**, Alvis J. 130
**Hunter**, Theresa M. 137
**Hutcheson**, Hugh 142
**Hutchins**, Ralph 61

## I

**Innis**, Tangela U. 137
**Irwin**, Mark D. 131

## J

**James**, Erik R. 131
**Jefferson**, Christopher C. 131
**Jenkins** 27, Joseph 123
**Jennings**, Luther H. 138
**Jewell**, D. 93, Darl W. 125
**Johnson**, Anthony G. Sr. 131, D.D.C. 143, Durrell R. 131, Gregory M. 125, James V. 131, Lenhard R. 131, T. R. 10, Walter L. 125
**Johnston**, T. R. 25
**Jones**, Anthony 107, 125, C. C. 11, L. S. 25, 106, Ronnie P. 131, Shawn 7, 105, 125, William C. Jr. 131, William E. 138
**Joynes**, William H. 16

## K

**Karabulut**, Erdal 131
**Kersey**, Warren W. 59, William W. 61
**Khabir**, Samad A. 131
**Knight**, Kevin A. 131, Larry D. 131
**Kofie**, Pope J. 131
**Kuper**, John S. III 131
**Kyger**, Kyle L. 125

## L

**Labadie**, Sean M. 131
**Lambert**, Bobby E. 138, Courtland A. Jr. 131
**Law**, Bryan 125

150

# INDEX

**Lawrence**, Wallace H. Jr. 138
**Lawson**, Jeffrey L. 131, John W. 131
**Ledbetter**, Phillips S. 131
**Lee**, Clifton 131
**Legeros**, Mike 7
**Levy**, Ash 142
**Lewis**, Bernard C. 59, 61, Clarence E. III 125, Clinton M. 131, Gary R. Jr. 131, Jerry 149, Richard D. Jr. 125, Ronald C. 17, 29
**Little**, Donnie L. 131
**Liverman** 117, Melvin V. III 125
**Longest**, N.Y. 68
**Loving**, David M. 131
**Lucas**, Farrar 59
**Lukhard**, John T. 131

## M

**Maass**, Robert T. 131
**Mack**, William C. 131
**Madison**, Julian E. 138
**Mangum** 142
**Mann**, John H. 10
**Martin**, Bailey C. Jr. 125, Jason P. 131, M. 111, Mike 112, William M. 125
**Mary**, Joseph A. 131
**Marziale**, Peter J. 132
**Mason**, James 142
**Matt**, W. C. 10
**Maury**, R. H. Jr. 142
**Mayhew**, Kouri R. 132
**Mayo**, William 19
**McCain**, James A. 132
**McCall**, George L. Jr. 132
**McCarter**, Phillip A. 132, Robin C. 125
**McCarthy**, William J. 132
**McCarty**, William B. 132
**McCloud**, Lupe M. 132
**McCormick**, Michael E. 132
**McElfish**, Jack K. 17, 38
**McFarland**, William A. 132
**McGirt**, Terry L. 125
**McGovern**, Shawn P. 132
**McIntyre**, Jack R. 132
**McKearin**, Francis J. III 132
**Meadors** 25
**Melchek**, John J. 132
**Menon**, Mini G. 137
**Meredith** 142
**Mesco**, Adam C. 132, Eric R. 132, Leo A. Jr. 132
**Mezera**, Charles P. 132
**Milby**, Terry L. 132
**Miller**, G. W. 12, Michael G. 132
**Mingee**, G. D. 12
**Minter**, Arthur R. Jr. 132
**Moore**, Christopher J. 132, Jody T. 132
**Moran**, Marshall P. 132
**Morris**, Christopher A. 137, Orlando L. 113, 125
**Mullen**, Frank L. 16
**Mundie**, Gregory K. 132
**Murray**, Benjamin P. 132
**Murrin**, Michael W. 132
**Myers**, Robert L. 61, Roger R. Jr. 5, 6, 7, 8, 132

## N

**Nash**, M. B. 10
**Nelsen**, James E. 125
**Nelson**, Reginold R. 132
**Neville**, Hallie T. 125, Laura P. 132, Raymond N. 125
**Newcomb**, Wayne P. 133
**Nicholson**, Douglas D. 138
**Niver**, Mary Beth 137
**Nixon**, Steven W. 125
**Norment**, Richard M. 10, 143
**Nunnally**, Richard A. Jr. 133

## O

**Odell**, W. R. 10, 143
**Oprandy**, Michael A. 125
**Owens**, Daniel T. 133, Mark W. 133
**Oyler**, Nathan C. 133

## P

**Page**, Arthur L. 59, 61
**Parker**, Robert W. 133
**Patterson**, R. A. 143
**Peddicord**, Patrick J. 125
**Pegram**, Thomas H. 9
**Perdue**, William J. 7
**Perry**, D'Jalmar A. 133, Ronald R. 133
**Pettiford**, Korey L. 133
**Plaskett**, Lawrence E. Jr. 133
**Polifka**, Donald K. Jr. 125
**Pollard**, Craig W. 133
**Poole**, William C. 138
**Portwood**, Wilton V. 133
**Possanza**, Michael L. 133
**Potter**, Jamie L. 133
**Powell**, Michael W. 125
**Pratt**, Timothy W. 133
**Preau**, Travis L. 125
**Pritchett**, Kennard 133
**Puller** 23, W. G. 16
**Pulliam**, David D. Jr. 123

## R

**Rada**, Mark V. 125
**Ragsdale**, Steven W. 133
**Reamey**, James C. 133
**Reintz**, Charles H. 9
**Rice**, Anthony M. 133, Brian K. 133, William M. 133
**Richardson** 144, Christine 125, D. C. 144, G. C. 10, 25, Stephen B. 126
**Riddell**, William J. 133
**Riley**, Percy L. Jr. 13, Sean P. 133
**Ring**, Harold B. 126
**Rippy**, Darnell J. 133
**Rivers** 148, Robert L. Jr. 133
**Roberts** 113, A. 111, Andre R. 126, Kimberly M. 133, Powhattan 142
**Robertson**, Bruce D. 133
**Robinson**, Frederick J. 59, 61
**Ross**, David M. 126
**Rosser**, Ricky L. 126
**Ruffin**, Melvin L. 133
**Runion**, David H. 133
**Russ**, Melissa A. 126
**Rutherford**, T. M. 143
**Ryals**, Mark K. 133
**Ryan**, Stephen J. 134

## S

**Salim**, Jabari O. 134
**Salotti**, Don A. 126
**Satchell**, Melvin D. 134
**Satterwhite**, Lloyd D. 134
**Scales**, Jay S. Jr. 134, Jay S. Sr. 134
**Schmidt**, Joseph R. 134
**Schoeffel**, Patrick M. 7, 126
**Schoenhut**, Scott E. 123
**Schofield**, Wheeler 142
**Seal**, Douglas S. 134
**Seay**, James L. Jr. 134
**Sessions**, Clephos Sr. 134, Floyd N. Sr. 134
**Shaughnessy**, Bland E. 138
**Shaw**, George C. 9, 16
**Shears**, Charles K. 134
**Shelton**, Donald N. 126
**Sherry**, Edgar A. 17
**Shires**, Donald 134
**Short**, Ronald A. 134
**Shortt**, Gary W. 126
**Shulleeta**, William A. 134
**Signorelli**, Joseph J. 134
**Siguenza**, Marco R. 134
**Simon**, Patrick J. 134
**Sims**, Otis L. 134
**Slater**, Stratford L. Jr. 134
**Smith**, Barry G. 134, Carroll 7, 126, Christina H. 137, Claude F. Jr. 126, Michael E. Jr. 134, Shaundell L. 134, T. P. 143, Warren A. 138, William T. 134
**Southers**, Ross A. Jr. 138
**Spanbauer**, John P. 126
**Spencer**, Christopher W. 134
**Spindle**, William T. III 134
**Spivey**, Melody C. 126
**Spruill**, Kevin T. 126, Rodney 134
**Squire**, Terrence T. 134
**Stallings**, Michael J. 134
**Sterling**, Reginald K. 138
**Stevens**, Billy 120, Scott D. 134
**Stevenson**, Dewarren K. 135
**Stewart**, Adam M. 135, Patrick M. 135
**Stinson**, Elton F. 135
**St. John**, Arthur C. 59, 61
**Stokes** 148, Edward B. 135
**Stowell**, Charles U. III 135, Charles U. Jr. 126, Christopher W. 135, Kellie Andes 135
**Strybing**, Christopher 135
**Swanson**, G. 12

## T

**Talley**, William R. 126
**Taylor**, A. F. 16, Elmond D. 122, George III 135, G. Watt 16, 23, Kent O. Sr. 123, Wesley 7
**Thiel**, Stewart 7, 135
**Thomas**, J. N. 12
**Thomas**, Tracy A. 123
**Thompson** 118
**Throckmorton**, Michael L. 135
**Todd**, Lee A. 135
**Toepke**, Blake L. 126
**Townes**, Kenneth L. 126
**Trent**, John A. 135
**Trimble**, Charles C. 135
**Trimiew**, Alonzo E. Sr. 135
**Tunstall**, Larry R. 18
**Turnage**, Brian C. 126
**Turner**, James C. 135
**Turpin**, Steven L. 135
**Tyler**, Wayne P. 135

## V

**Verlander**, James E. 135
**Vida**, Keith 6, 7, 107, 126, Kimberli Russ 7
**VonMille**, Paul M. 135
**Vytlacil**, William 126

## W

**Waddy**, Chadwick S. 135
**Wade**, Calvin 61
**Wagner**, Mark O. 126
**Waldron**, Daniel 7, 135
**Walker** 142, James W. 126, Rodger 7, 135
**Wall**, Robert W. 135
**Walton**, Ronald N. 135
**Waltrip**, Linwood L. II 135
**Ware**, Pat 120, William K. 135
**Washington**, Norman E. 135, Ronald T. Sr. 135
**Waters**, Brion N. 136
**Watkins**, Mark W. 136, Tina 109, 126
**Watson**, Charles 142, Michael E. 136
**Watts**, Larry F. 136
**Weaver** 26
**Webb**, Lewis N. 142
**Wegner**, Steven K. 136
**Wells** 142, Anthony 7, 136, Christopher D. 136
**West**, Bobby R. 127, Kenneth W. Sr. 136
**Weymouth** 148, Garland W. 127
**White**, Joseph D. 136
**Whiteley**, Shaun T. 136
**Whitlock**, Kevin N. 136
**Wilder**, L. Douglas 18
**Wilkerson**, Barry M. 136
**Wilkins**, Michael T. 136
**Williams**, Gui J. 136, Jerry W. 127, Joan Draucker 138, John M. 136, Sheldon L. 127, T. C. 143, Terrance I. 136, Thelburt A. 136, Thomas L. 136, Tyrelle C. 136
**Williamson**, Steven W. 136
**Wilson-Cho**, Kimberly 105, 137
**Winston**, Marlon R. 136
**Witherspoon**, Robert C. 136
**Woodcock**, Robert A. 138
**Wood**, Everett B. 136, S. J. 11
**Woodward** 9
**Wooldridge**, Linwood M. 59, 60
**Wright**, David L. Sr. 136, E. M. 9, Fred D. 127, Neale P. 136
**Wyatt**, G. L. 12

151

# FireFighter's Career History

**Name** _____

**Date of Hire** _____

**Date of Retirement** _____

| ASSIGNMENTS | AWARDS/PROMOTIONS |
|---|---|
| _____ | _____ |
| _____ | _____ |
| _____ | _____ |
| _____ | _____ |
| _____ | _____ |
| _____ | _____ |
| _____ | _____ |
| _____ | _____ |
| _____ | _____ |
| _____ | _____ |
| _____ | _____ |
| _____ | _____ |
| _____ | _____ |
| _____ | _____ |

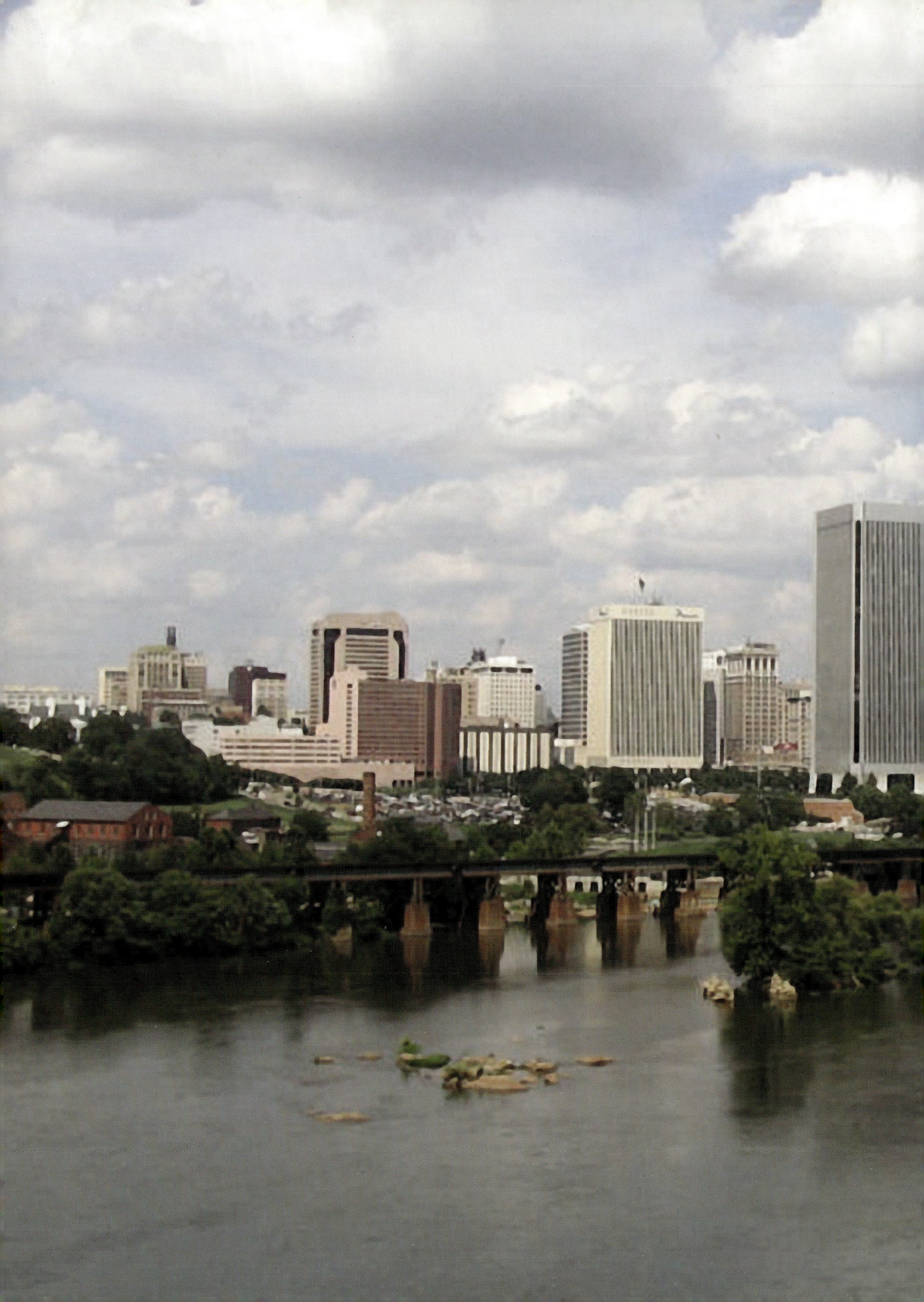